FOOLPROOF

Family Recipes

Gooseberry Patch

An imprint of Globe Pequot
246 Goose Lane
Guilford, CT 06437

www.gooseberrypatch.com
1•800•854•6673

Copyright 2014, Gooseberry Patch 978-1-62093-145-5

Do you have a tried & true recipe...

tip, craft or memory that you'd like to see featured in
a **Gooseberry Patch** cookbook? Visit our website at
www.gooseberrypatch.com, register and follow the
easy steps to submit your favorite family recipe.
Or send them to us at:

Gooseberry Patch
PO Box 812
Columbus, OH 43216-0812

Don't forget to include the number of servings your recipe makes,
plus your name, address, phone number and email address. If we
select your recipe, your name will appear right along with it...
and you'll receive a **FREE** copy of the book!

CONTENTS

DEDICATION

Dedicated to everyone
who agrees that the
most satisfying meals
are made with a secret
ingredient...love!

APPRECIATION

Our heartiest thanks to
all of you who opened
your recipe boxes to
share tried & true
recipes with us.

BREAKFAST & BRUNCH Delights

Buttermilk

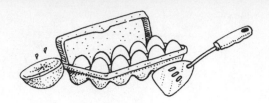

Cheesy Scrambled Eggs

Kathy Grashoff
Fort Wayne, IN

A skillet full of breakfast goodness! Finely chopped ham or sliced mushrooms may be added...cook them in the butter for a few minutes before pouring in the eggs.

8 eggs	1/8 t. pepper
1/2 c. shredded Cheddar cheese	2 to 4 T. butter, sliced
1/8 t. salt	

In a large bowl, whisk eggs to break up yolks. Add cheese, salt and pepper, whisking until well blended; set aside. Melt butter in a large skillet over medium-low heat. Add egg mixture to skillet. Cook, stirring frequently, until eggs form soft, creamy curds. Serve immediately. Serves 4.

Baked Eggs & Cheese

Barb Rudyk
Vermilion, Alberta

A delicious breakfast casserole with just a few ingredients.

1/2 c. shredded Cheddar cheese	1 t. dry mustard
8 eggs	1/2 t. salt
1/2 c. whipping cream	1/2 t. pepper

Sprinkle cheese evenly in a greased 8"x8" baking pan; set aside. In a large bowl, whisk together remaining ingredients; pour evenly over cheese. Bake, uncovered, at 350 degrees for 30 minutes, or until eggs are set. Serve immediately. Serves 4.

Broiled tomatoes are a tasty, quick garnish for eggs. Place tomato halves on a broiler pan, cut-side up. Drizzle tomatoes lightly with olive oil; season with salt and pepper. Broil tomatoes until tender, 2 to 3 minutes.

Peppy Potato Pancakes

Tina George
El Dorado, AR

*These savory pancakes are perfect for breakfast or dinner.
Enjoy them as a perfect side to a simple meal, topped with
a dollop of applesauce or sour cream.*

2 eggs
1/2 c. onion, halved and sliced
2 potatoes, peeled and cut into
   1-inch cubes

1/2 t. salt
1/8 t. cayenne pepper
3 T. all-purpose flour
4 T. oil, divided

Place eggs and onion in a blender; cover and process until blended. Add potatoes; cover and process until finely chopped. Pour mixture into a bowl. Stir in salt, cayenne pepper and flour, adding a little more flour if batter is too thin; set aside. Heat 2 tablespoons oil in a large non-stick skillet over medium heat. Drop batter into oil by 1/4 cupfuls, making 4 pancakes. Cook until pancakes are golden on the bottom; turn and cook until golden on other side. Repeat with remaining batter, adding more oil as necessary. Drain on paper towels. Serves 4.

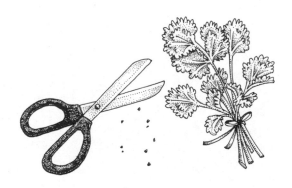

Fresh herbs add savor and color to breakfast dishes...simply snip
herbs directly into eggs or potatoes as they cook. Some herbs to
try include chives, dill, thyme and parsley.

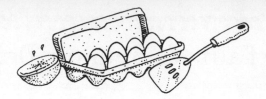

Eggs in a Nest

Laura Fuller
Fort Wayne, IN

A fun and satisfying breakfast from way back...
kids of all ages love it!

2 slices white bread
2 T. butter, sliced
2 eggs

salt and pepper to taste
Optional: catsup

Use a 2-1/2" round cookie cutter to cut out the center of each bread slice. Save cut-out circles; set aside. Melt butter in a skillet over medium heat; add bread slices and circles to skillet. Crack an egg into the center of each bread slice, being careful not to break the yolks. Season with salt and pepper. Cook until bread slices are golden on the bottom, about 3 to 4 minutes. Carefully turn over slices and circles with a spatula; cook on other side until eggs are set to desired doneness, one to 2 minutes. Top each egg with a toast circle. Serve with catsup, if desired. Makes 2 servings.

Salt & pepper are a must for eggs and potatoes at breakfast.
It's the perfect time to show off a pair of vintage shakers
in whimsical shapes.

Savory Egg Strata

Michelle Blair-Weeks
Santa Rosa, CA

This is a great versatile brunch dish. Put it together the night before, then bake it in the morning...so convenient.

6 to 8 slices bread, toasted
   and crusts trimmed
10 eggs
1-3/4 c. milk
salt and pepper to taste

2-1/2 c. cooked sausage, ham
   or bacon, chopped
1 c. shredded Cheddar, Monterey
   Jack or American cheese

The night before, arrange toast slices in the bottom of a buttered 13"x9" baking pan; set aside. In a large bowl, beat together eggs, milk, salt and pepper; pour over toast. Sprinkle meat and cheese over egg mixture. Cover and refrigerate for 8 hours to overnight. In the morning, let stand at room temperature for 15 to 20 minutes. Uncover and bake at 350 degrees for 30 minutes, or until eggs are set and cheese is melted. Makes 8 servings.

Variation:

Spicy Egg Strata: Add a spoonful of canned diced green chiles to egg mixture. Use cooked chorizo sausage and Pepper Jack cheese. Prepare as directed above.

Looking ahead to a busy day tomorrow? Get your family's day off to a sunny start with an overnight breakfast dish like Savory Egg Strata that can be assembled the night before and just popped in the oven in the morning.

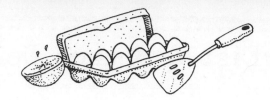

Blueberry Buttermilk Pancakes

JoyceAnn Dreibelbis
Wooster, OH

Pure maple syrup is the perfect partner for these delicious golden pancakes. When fresh blueberries aren't available, you can use frozen berries...no need to thaw, just add to the batter.

3 T. butter, melted and slightly
    cooled
1 c. buttermilk
1 egg
2 t. lemon zest
3/4 c. all-purpose flour, or
    1/2 c. all-purpose flour plus
    1/4 c. whole-wheat flour

1 t. baking soda
1/2 t. cinnamon
1-1/2 c. blueberries
Optional: 1/2 c. chopped walnuts
Garnish: maple syrup

In a small bowl, whisk together butter, buttermilk, egg and lemon zest; set aside. In a larger bowl, whisk together flour, baking soda and cinnamon. Whisk butter mixture into flour mixture until batter is smooth. Lightly spray a griddle with non-stick vegetable spray; heat griddle over medium heat. Ladle batter onto griddle by 1/2 cupfuls. Sprinkle each pancake with 2 tablespoons blueberries and one tablespoon walnuts, if desired. Cook until pancakes are golden on the bottom. Turn carefully and cook until golden on other side, about 2 minutes more. Serve with maple syrup. Makes about one dozen pancakes.

Here's how to tell when a pancake griddle is hot enough for the batter... just sprinkle a little water on it. If it sizzles, the griddle is ready to go.

German Apple Pancake

Carmen Graham
Albuquerque, NM

Being of German descent, I like to try recipes that look like they might be from Germany. Of course this one caught my eye. I made a few adjustments to it...my husband just loves it! Serve with sausage links or patties.

2 T. butter
2 to 3 Granny Smith apples,
   cored and sliced
4 eggs
3/4 c. milk

3/4 c. all-purpose flour
1/2 t. salt
Garnish: powdered sugar,
   lemon wedges

Place butter in a 10" ovenproof skillet or pie plate. Place pan in oven at 450 degrees until butter melts. Arrange sliced apples over melted butter; set aside. In a bowl, beat eggs well. Add milk, flour and salt; beat until smooth. Pour batter over apples. Reduce oven to 350 degrees. Bake until crisp and golden, 45 to 60 minutes. Cut into wedges; serve warm with powdered sugar and/or lemon wedges. Serves 4 to 6.

A top tip for success in the kitchen: read through the recipe first!
Make sure you have all the ingredients, equipment and time needed
to make the recipe. You'll be glad you did!

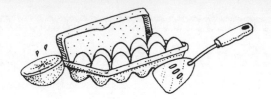

Granola Crunch Pancakes

*Sue Klapper
Muskego, WI*

Crush granola between sheets of waxed paper with a rolling pin.

2 c. pancake mix
1-1/2 c. milk
2 eggs, beaten

2 T. oil
1 c. granola cereal, crushed

In a bowl, whisk together pancake mix, milk, eggs and oil until smooth. Spray a griddle with non-stick vegetable spray; heat over medium heat. Pour batter onto griddle by 1/4 cupfuls; sprinkle each pancake with 2 tablespoons granola. Cook until bubbly on the surface and golden on the bottom. Turn and cook until other side is golden. Makes 7 to 8 pancakes.

Variations:

Apple-Cinnamon Pancakes: Omit granola. Toss one cup peeled and cored apple, thinly sliced, with one tablespoon sugar and one teaspoon cinnamon. Prepare as above, adding apple instead of granola.

Spiced Peach Pancakes: Omit granola. Toss one cup chopped canned peaches with one teaspoon cinnamon. Prepare as above, adding peaches instead of granola.

Cranberry Pancakes: Omit granola. Toss one cup chopped fresh cranberries with 2 tablespoons sugar. Prepare as above, adding cranberries instead of granola.

For light, tender pancakes, replace some of the liquid in the recipe with club soda. Stir it in at the last minute, just before pouring batter onto the hot griddle.

Upside-Down Orange French Toast

Angie Venable
Gooseberry Patch

With this recipe, you can bake up a panful of
luscious French toast in a jiffy!

1/4 c. butter, sliced	4 eggs
1/3 c. sugar	2/3 c. orange juice
1/4 t. cinnamon	8 slices firm white bread
1 t. orange zest	

Place butter in a 15"x10" jelly-roll pan. Place pan in oven at 325 degrees until butter melts; set aside. In a shallow bowl, mix together sugar, cinnamon and orange zest; sprinkle mixture over melted butter. In a separate shallow bowl, whisk together eggs and juice. Dip bread into egg mixture, soaking well. Arrange bread in pan on top of sugar mixture. Bake at 325 degrees for 20 minutes, or until golden, watching carefully to avoid burning. Lift out toast slices and flip over onto plates. Makes 8 slices.

Fresh eggs can safely be kept refrigerated for 4 to 5 weeks, so go ahead and stock up when they're on sale. Store eggs in their carton to prevent them from absorbing odors from other foods...preferably in the coldest part of the fridge, not the egg tray on the door.

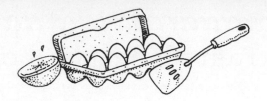

Mushroom & Herb Omelet

Penny Sherman
Saint Louis, MO

Don't worry if the omelet splits or tears as the edges are lifted...
the cheese topping will make it look and taste delicious!

2 eggs
1-1/2 t. fresh parsley, snipped
1/2 t. fresh thyme, basil or
   chives, snipped
salt and pepper to taste

3/4 c. sliced mushrooms
2 t. butter, divided
1 to 2 T. shredded Swiss or
   Cheddar cheese

Whisk together eggs, herbs, salt and pepper in a small bowl; set aside. In a small skillet over medium heat, sauté mushrooms in one teaspoon butter until tender, 3 to 4 minutes. Transfer mushrooms to a separate bowl; cover and set aside. Melt remaining butter in skillet; pour egg mixture into skillet. Cook over medium-low heat, lifting edge gently with a spatula to allow uncooked portion to flow underneath. When almost set, spoon mushrooms onto one half of the omelet; fold over omelet. Sprinkle with cheese; let stand one to 2 minutes until cheese melts. Slide onto a plate. Serves one.

Egg dishes are a perfect way to use up tasty tidbits from the fridge...
ham, bacon and chopped veggies. Warm briefly in a skillet
and set aside for an omelet filling, or scramble the eggs right in.

Denver Scramble

Kathleen Kennedy
Renton, WA

All my menfolk love this dish! The recipe can easily be divided or multiplied depending on how many hungry diners you have. Add fresh fruit and buttered toast for a well-rounded meal.

3 to 4 T. butter
1 lb. thick-sliced cooked deli
    ham, diced
1 c. green or red peppers, diced
1 c. yellow onion, diced

6 eggs
1/4 c. milk
pepper to taste
1/2 c. shredded Cheddar cheese
Optional: diced tomatoes

Melt butter in a large skillet over medium heat until it starts to sizzle. Add ham, peppers and onion to skillet; cook until vegetables are crisp-tender. Meanwhile, whisk together eggs and milk in a bowl. Stir egg mixture into mixture in skillet; season with pepper. Reduce heat to medium-low. Cook until eggs are set, stirring occasionally, 4 to 5 minutes. Remove skillet from heat. Top with cheese; let stand for a minute, until cheese melts. Sprinkle with tomatoes, if desired. Serves 4 to 6.

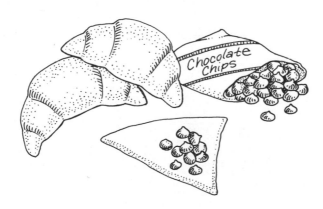

Chocolate croissants in a jiffy! Unroll a tube of refrigerated crescent dough and separate it into triangles. Top each triangle with 10 chocolate chips and roll it up. Place triangles on an ungreased baking sheet. Bake at 375 degrees until golden, 12 to 14 minutes. Serve warm.

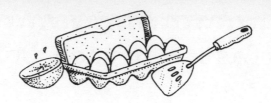

Alice's Breakfast Egg Pizza

Barbara Spilsbury
Heber City, UT

This recipe was shared with me by a dear old friend who recently passed away. She was a great cook. Garnish your pizza with salsa, sliced avocado or anything you desire.

1 lb. ground pork breakfast
   sausage
8-oz. tube refrigerated crescent
   rolls
1 c. frozen diced potatoes,
   thawed
1 c. shredded Cheddar, Swiss or
   Monterey Jack cheese

5 eggs
1/4 c. milk
1/2 t. salt
1/8 t. pepper
2 T. grated Parmesan cheese

In a microwave-safe dish, microwave sausage for about 6 minutes, until browned; drain well. Sausage may also be browned in a skillet. Meanwhile, unroll rolls without separating them. Press rolls into a 12" round pizza pan, forming a crust. Spoon sausage, potatoes and shredded cheese over crust. In a bowl, beat together eggs, milk, salt and pepper; spoon over top. Sprinkle with Parmesan cheese. Bake at 375 degrees for 25 to 30 minutes, until crust is golden and cheese is melted. Cut into wedges. Makes 8 servings.

Make school-day breakfasts fun! Along with Breakfast Egg Pizza, serve milk with twisty straws and skewers of juicy strawberries and orange slices.

Cheesy Hashbrown Casserole

Crystal MacLean
Camrose, Alberta

My mom always made this casserole for our Christmas breakfast. She would slip it into into the oven when we awoke to open our stockings. Such a delicious memory!

4 c. frozen diced potatoes
1 c. sour cream
10-3/4 oz. can cream of
    mushroom soup
2 c. shredded Cheddar cheese

1/8 t. pepper
Optional: 1 T. onion, finely
    chopped
Garnish: grated Parmesan
    cheese

In a large bowl, mix together all ingredients except garnish. Spoon into a greased 8"x8" glass baking pan. Sprinkle lightly with Parmesan cheese. Bake, uncovered, at 350 degrees for one hour, or until center is hot and sides are bubbly. May also be made a day ahead, covered and refrigerated, then baked in the morning. Serves 6.

Better-Than-Plain Hashbrowns

Nancy Romero
Rayne, LA

One day I had such a craving for good hashbrowns and had company wanting true Cajun cooking. So I came up with this compromise...they loved it and so do I!

8 slices bacon
1/2 c. onion, chopped
1/2 c. green pepper, chopped

16-oz. pkg. frozen diced
    potatoes
salt and pepper to taste

In a large skillet over medium heat, cook bacon until crisp. Remove bacon to a paper towel; reserve 2 tablespoons drippings in skillet. Sauté onion and green pepper in drippings until softened. Add potatoes, salt and pepper; stir to blend. Cook potatoes according to package directions, turning occasionally, until tender and golden. Stir in crumbled bacon. Serves 4 to 6.

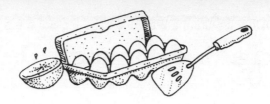

Fall French Toast

Laura Hill-Lindquist
Anchorage, AK

One morning I decided to spice up our French toast, and it became a hit! I love to make this recipe in chilly weather but it tastes good anytime. Hope you enjoy it as much as we do.

4 eggs	1/8 t. cinnamon
1 c. milk	1/8 t. nutmeg
1 T. vanilla extract	2 to 3 T. butter, divided
1 t. sugar	10 to 12 slices bread
1/8 t. pumpkin pie spice	Garnish: butter, maple syrup

In a shallow bowl, beat together eggs, milk, vanilla, sugar and spices. Heat a griddle or skillet over medium heat with a small amount of butter. Add one bread slice to egg mixture; let stand for a few seconds, then turn to coat the other side. Place coated slice of bread on griddle and cook until golden; turn and cook other side until golden. Repeat with remaining slices, adding more butter as needed. Serve warm with additional butter and syrup. Makes 10 to 12 slices.

Honey Butter

Hope Davenport
Portland, TX

Delicious slathered on warm pancakes, waffles, toast or muffins! It is so simple to whip up and keeps well in the fridge.

1/2 c. butter, room temperature	1/2 t. cinnamon
2 T. honey	

Blend all ingredients in a bowl. Cover and refrigerate. Makes 1/2 cup.

Set aside day-old bread for making French toast...it absorbs the milk so much better than bakery-fresh bread.

Angel Fluff Waffles

Wendy Jo Minotte
Duluth, MN

This is our family's all-time favorite waffle. Served with butter and maple syrup or strawberry butter, it's an extra special breakfast. These waffles freeze well and may be reheated in the microwave.

2 eggs, separated
1/4 c. white vinegar
1-3/4 c. milk
1/3 c. oil

2 c. all-purpose flour
1 T. sugar
1 t. baking soda
1/2 t. salt

In a small bowl, beat egg whites with an electric mixer on high speed until stiff peaks form; set aside. In a large bowl, beat together egg yolks, vinegar, milk and oil. In a separate bowl, whisk together remaining ingredients; add to egg yolk mixture. Carefully fold egg whites into batter. For each waffle, pour 1/2 cup batter onto a heated and greased waffle iron. Bake according to manufacturer's instructions. Makes 7 waffles.

Strawberry Butter

Kim Hinshaw
Cedar Park, TX

Serve on hot waffles, biscuits, breads or rolls.

12-oz. container fresh
   strawberries, hulled

1 c. butter, room temperature
1/2 c. powdered sugar

Process strawberries in a food processor until smooth; set aside. In a large bowl, beat butter with an electric mixer on high speed until light and fluffy. Add strawberries and powdered sugar; blend thoroughly. Keep refrigerated in a covered container. Makes about 3 cups.

If part of a broken eggshell makes its way into the waffle or pancake batter, just dip a clean eggshell into the batter. The broken one will grab onto it like a magnet.

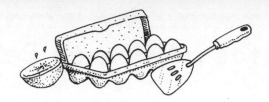

Sour Cream Coffee Cake

Mariann Raferty
New Rochelle, NY

This is the very first recipe that fed my passion for baking...it is like a comforting friend. Looks so special in a Bundt® pan!

1/2 c. butter, softened
1/2 c. margarine, softened
1-1/4 c. sugar
2 eggs
1 c. sour cream, room
    temperature
2 c. all-purpose flour
1-1/2 t. baking powder

1/2 t. baking soda
3/4 c. chopped walnuts
1/2 c. mini semi-sweet chocolate
    chips
2 T. brown sugar, packed
1-1/2 t. cinnamon
1/4 t. nutmeg
Garnish: powdered sugar

In a bowl, blend together butter, margarine and sugar. Add eggs and sour cream; beat well. In a separate bowl, stir together flour, baking powder and baking soda. Gradually add flour mixture to butter mixture; stir with a wooden spoon until batter is well mixed. In a small bowl, mix walnuts, chocolate chips, brown sugar and spices. Spoon half of batter into a greased 10" Bundt® pan. Sprinkle half of walnut mixture over batter. Add remaining batter; top with remaining walnut mixture. Bake at 350 degrees for 45 minutes, or until a toothpick inserted near the center tests clean. Cool cake in pan for 10 to 20 minutes. Loosen cake around the edges with a butter knife; turn out cake onto a wire rack and cool completely. At serving time, sprinkle cake with powdered sugar. Makes 8 to 10 servings.

Serve hot spiced coffee with fresh-baked coffee cake. Simply add 3/4 teaspoon apple pie spice to 1/2 cup ground coffee and brew as usual.

Lemon-Blueberry Coffee Cake

Jennifer Fox
Fredericktown, OH

This is a tried & true favorite of my family...the combination of the lemon and blueberry is oh-so good! Delicious served warm or cooled.

18-1/4 oz. pkg. lemon cake mix
1/2 c. butter, softened
2 eggs

2/3 c. milk
1 c. fresh or frozen blueberries

In a large bowl, combine dry cake mix and butter; mix until crumbly. Set aside 1-1/4 cups of crumb mixture for topping. To remaining crumb mixture, add eggs and milk. Beat with an electric mixer on medium speed for 2 minutes. Spread batter in a greased and floured 13"x9" baking pan. Top with fresh or frozen berries and reserved crumb mixture. Bake at 325 degrees for 25 to 30 minutes. Serve warm or cooled. Makes 10 to 12 servings.

When whisking or beating ingredients in a bowl, a damp kitchen towel can keep the mixing bowl in place. Just twist the towel securely around the base of the bowl.

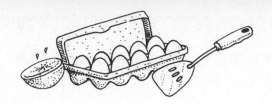

Overnight Cherry Danish

Amanda Holman
Bemidji, MN

I remember my grandmum making Danishes with all of the grandchildren every year on the day before Christmas Eve. She would give each of us a part of the recipe to do...such fun! The recipe may look complicated, but it really isn't.

2 envs. active dry yeast
1/2 c. warm milk, 110 to
   115 degrees
6 c. all-purpose flour
1/3 c. sugar
2 t. salt

1 c. cold butter, cubed
1-1/2 c. warm half-and-half,
   110 to 115 degrees
6 egg yolks, lightly beaten
21-oz. can cherry pie filling

In a small bowl, dissolve yeast in warm milk; set aside. In a large bowl, combine flour, sugar and salt; cut in butter with 2 knives until crumbly. Add yeast mixture, warm half-and-half and egg yolks; stir until a soft, sticky dough forms. Cover with a tea towel and refrigerate overnight. The next day, punch down dough; divide into 4 portions. On a floured surface, roll each portion into an 18-inch by 4-inch rectangle; cut into 4-inch by one-inch strips. Place 2 strips side-by-side; twist together. Shape into a ring; pinch ends together. Repeat with remaining strips. Place rolls 2 inches apart on greased baking sheets. Cover with a tea towel. Let rise in a warm place until double, about 45 minutes. Using the end of a wooden spoon handle, make a 1/2-inch deep indentation in the center of each roll. Fill each with one tablespoon pie filling. Bake at 350 degrees for 14 to 16 minutes, until lightly golden. Remove from pans to wire racks to cool. Drizzle rolls with Powdered Sugar Icing. Makes 3 dozen.

Powdered Sugar Icing:

2 T. butter, softened
3 c. powdered sugar
1/4 t. vanilla extract

1/8 t. salt
4 to 5 T. half-and-half

In a large bowl, beat butter until fluffy. Gradually beat in powdered sugar, vanilla, salt and enough half-and-half to make a drizzling consistency.

Cinnamon-Orange Pull-Aparts

Shannon Reents
Loudonville, OH

This recipe was given to me by a very dear friend, known to my husband as his second mother. It's a sweet twist on the popular recipe called Monkey Bread.

18 frozen bread dough rolls
3/4 c. sugar
1-1/2 t. cinnamon

1 t. orange zest
5 T. butter, melted
1/3 c. light corn syrup, divided

Thaw rolls according to package directions; cut in half. In a shallow bowl, combine sugar, cinnamon and orange zest; mix well. Place melted butter in a separate shallow bowl. Dip half of the cut rolls into butter; roll in sugar mixture to coat. Arrange rolls in a 10" Bundt® pan sprayed with non-stick vegetable spray. Drizzle rolls with half the corn syrup. Repeat with remaining rolls and syrup; sprinkle any remaining sugar mixture over rolls. Cover loosely with plastic wrap and a tea towel. Let rise in a warm place until double in bulk, about one hour. Uncover; bake at 350 degrees for 30 to 35 minutes, until top is deeply golden. Cool in pan on a wire rack for 5 minutes. Carefully invert rolls onto a serving plate. To serve, pull apart or slice. Makes 1-1/2 dozen.

For best results when baking, preheat the oven first. Turn on the oven and set it to the correct temperature at least 15 minutes ahead of time.

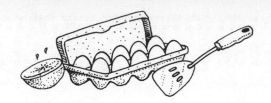

Peachy Baked Oatmeal

Hannah Hilgendorf
Nashotah, WI

*I found this recipe and tweaked it until it was just right for us.
It was an instant hit! It's also yummy made with cranberry
chutney or other mostly-firm fruit instead of peaches.*

2 eggs, beaten
1/2 c. brown sugar, packed
1-1/2 t. baking powder
1/4 t. salt
1-1/2 t. cinnamon
1/2 t. nutmeg
1-1/2 t. vanilla extract

3/4 c. milk
3 c. long-cooking oats,
   uncooked
1/3 c. oil
16-oz. can sliced peaches,
   partially drained
Garnish: warm milk

In a bowl, combine eggs, brown sugar, baking powder, salt, spices
and vanilla; beat well. Add remaining ingredients except garnish;
mix thoroughly. Spoon into a greased 8"x8" baking pan. Bake at
375 degrees for 20 to 25 minutes, until center is set. Serve in bowls,
topped with warm milk. Serves 6.

The greatest sweetener of human life is friendship.
– Joseph Addison

Sandi's Special Apple Oatmeal

Sandra Leasure
Circleville, OH

An easy-to-make breakfast treat! If you like thicker oatmeal,
add a little more oats; for thinner, add more milk.

5 c. milk
3 c. whole-grain quick-cooking
    oats, uncooked
1-1/2 c. apples, peeled, cored
    and diced

1/2 c. light brown sugar, packed
1 t. cinnamon
Optional: milk, brown sugar

In a heavy saucepan over medium heat, bring milk to a boil. Stir in
oats, apples, brown sugar and cinnamon. Cook for one minute, stirring
occasionally. Remove from heat; cover and let stand for 2 to
3 minutes. Serve topped with milk and additional brown sugar,
if desired. Makes 6 servings.

Plump raisins for extra flavor before adding them to oatmeal for
breakfast. Simply place the raisins in a bowl and cover with boiling water.
Soak for 15 minutes, drain and pat dry using a paper towel.

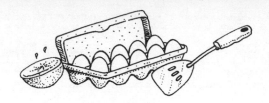

Sausage & Pecan Casserole

Elizabeth Smithson
Cunningham, KY

I found this recipe in my granny's cookbook many years ago. It's now a tradition at my family's annual brunch the first Saturday in December. We've been doing this for 12 years so far!

8-oz. pkg. pork breakfast
    sausage links
16-oz. loaf cinnamon bread,
    cubed
6 eggs, beaten
1-1/2 c. half-and-half

1-1/2 c. milk
1 t. vanilla extract
1 c. chopped pecans
1/2 t. cinnamon
1/2 t. nutmeg

Brown sausages in a skillet over medium heat; drain and thinly slice. Place bread cubes in a 13"x9" baking pan sprayed with non-stick vegetable spray. Top with sausages and set aside. In a bowl, beat together remaining ingredients. Pour egg mixture over sausage; press down gently. Cover and refrigerate overnight. In the morning, make Topping; sprinkle over top. Bake, uncovered, at 350 degrees for 35 minutes, or until bubbly and eggs are set. Serves 10.

Topping:

1 c. brown sugar, packed
1 c. chopped pecans

1/2 c. butter, softened
2 T. maple syrup

Stir together all ingredients with a fork until crumbly.

If weeknights are busy, why not enjoy a family brunch together on the weekend? Relax with each other over coffee and fruit juice, a basket of muffins and Sausage & Pecan Casserole. You'll be glad you did!

Home-Baked
BREADS

Bursting Blueberry Muffins

Kristie Rigo
Friedens, PA

I have tried many recipes for blueberry muffins, but these beat every other recipe, hands-down! They are perfect from crumbly top to berry-filled bottom. Make them extra special with cute paper muffin liners.

1/4 c. butter, softened	2 t. baking powder
3/4 c. sugar	1/2 c. milk
1 egg	2 c. fresh or frozen blueberries
2 c. all-purpose flour	

Blend butter and sugar in a large bowl; stir in egg and set aside. In a separate bowl, combine flour and baking powder. Add flour mixture to butter mixture alternately with milk; stir just until moistened. Fold in blueberries. Grease a 12-cup muffin tin or line with paper liners. Spoon batter into muffin cups, filling 2/3 full. Top evenly with Crumb Topping. Bake at 400 degrees for 20 to 25 minutes, until a toothpick inserted in the center tests clean. Allow muffins to cool in pan for 5 minutes; remove to a wire rack. Makes one dozen.

Crumb Topping:

1/4 c. butter, softened	1/2 c. all-purpose flour
1/2 c. sugar	1/2 t. cinnamon

Mix together all ingredients with a fork until crumbly.

A baker's secret! Grease muffin cups on the bottoms and just halfway up the sides...the muffins will bake up nicely puffed on top.

Sweet Potato Muffins

Lee-Ann Barnaby
Longueuil, Quebec

As a child, I used to love spending time with my grandmother and her best friend Ella. They would set up tea parties for me and make the most delicious baked goods, like these flavorful muffins. The recipe has been handed down through generations.

1-1/2 c. all-purpose flour
1 T. sugar
5 t. baking powder
1/2 t. salt
2 eggs
1 c. milk

1 c. cooked or canned sweet potatoes, mashed and strained
1/2 c. shortening, melted and slightly cooled

In a large bowl, stir together flour, sugar, baking powder and salt; set aside. Beat eggs in a separate bowl; whisk in milk. Add sweet potatoes; beat until smooth. Add flour mixture to sweet potato mixture; add shortening and stir just until moistened. Spoon batter into 15 muffin cups, filling 2/3 full. Bake at 400 degrees for 30 minutes, or until a toothpick inserted in the center tests clean. Serve warm. Makes 1-1/4 dozen.

Enjoy the taste of homemade muffins anytime. Freeze baked muffins in a freezer-safe bag, then just remove as many as needed and let thaw overnight in the fridge. To warm, wrap in aluminum foil and pop into a 300-degree oven for a few minutes.

Dreamy Orange Muffins

Brenda Huey
Geneva, IN

I love these muffins! They are moist and oh-so good. I make these for sale in my Cobblestone Bakery and they're a favorite.

8-oz. container orange-flavored
   yogurt
1 c. buttermilk
1-1/2 c. orange juice, divided
3 eggs
1 c. margarine, softened

1-1/2 c. sugar
2 T. baking powder
4 c. all-purpose flour
11-oz. can mandarin oranges,
   drained
2 c. powdered sugar

In a large bowl, combine yogurt, buttermilk, one cup orange juice, eggs, margarine and sugar. Stir until combined. Add baking powder and flour; mix just until combined. Stir in oranges. Grease a 12-cup muffin tin or line with paper liners. Fill muffin cups 2/3 full. Bake at 325 degrees for 20 to 25 minutes, or until a toothpick inserted in the center tests clean. Mix remaining orange juice with powdered sugar; drizzle over cooled muffins. Makes one dozen.

Get all the moms in the neighborhood together for a morning muffin swap! Ask everyone to bring a dozen muffins to share and some extras to sample. You'll have a fun time chatting and catching up on neighborhood happenings.

Strawberry Lemonade Muffins

Jackie Smulski
Lyons, IL

Try these muffins topped with strawberry jam...you'll love the combination of sweet and tart flavors.

2-1/2 c. self-rising flour
1-1/4 c. sugar, divided
8-oz. container sour cream
1/2 c. butter, melted and slightly
   cooled

2 eggs, lightly beaten
1 T. lemon zest
1/4 c. lemon juice
1-1/2 c. strawberries,
   hulled and diced

In a large bowl, combine flour and one cup sugar. Make a well in the center and set aside. In a separate bowl, stir together sour cream, butter, eggs, lemon zest and juice. Add sour cream mixture to flour mixture, stirring just until moistened. Gently fold strawberries into batter. Lightly grease a 12-cup muffin tin or line with paper liners. Spoon batter into muffin cups, filling 2/3 full. Sprinkle remaining sugar evenly over batter. Bake at 375 degrees for 16 to 18 minutes, until lightly golden and a toothpick inserted in the center tests clean. Cool muffins in tin for 5 minutes; transfer to a wire rack and cool completely. Makes one dozen.

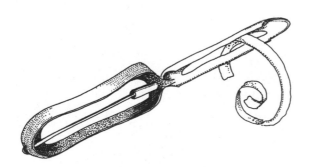

For lemon or orange zest in a jiffy, use a vegetable peeler to remove very thin slices of peel. Mince finely with a paring knife. Be sure to remove all of the bitter-tasting white pith.

Tea Scones

Mary Lou Jollymore
New Ross, Nova Scotia

I made these scones for my nephew's wedding luncheon, as they were having a traditional English Tea. I served them with my homemade strawberry jam...they were a great hit! I was asked for the recipe several times.

1-1/8 c. plus 1 t. milk, divided
1 t. white vinegar
3 c. all-purpose flour
3/4 c. sugar, divided
2 T. baking powder
1/2 t. salt
1/2 c. butter
1 egg
Garnish: butter, jam

Combine 1-1/8 cups milk and vinegar in a cup; set aside until soured, about 5 minutes. In a large bowl, stir together flour, 1/2 cup sugar, baking powder and salt. Cut in butter with 2 forks until crumbly. Add soured milk and stir gently. Turn dough out onto a floured surface. Gently knead together, dusting with flour if too moist. Form dough into a log and divide into 4 portions. Pat each portion into a circle, 1/2 to 3/4-inch thick; cut into 4 to 6 wedges. Arrange on parchment paper-lined baking sheets. Whisk together egg and remaining milk. Brush egg over scones and sprinkle with remaining sugar. Bake at 325 degrees for 30 minutes, or until golden. Serve warm with butter and jam. Makes 1-1/4 to 2 dozen.

Variation:

Berry Shortcakes: Split baked scones; serve topped with sweetened fresh berries and whipped cream.

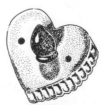

Add some love to a batch of Tea Scones. Pat out the dough, cut out with a heart-shaped cookie cutter and bake as usual. Drizzle with melted white chocolate...so pretty!

Cat's Cranberry-Orange Scones

Cathie Lopez
La Mirada, CA

I tasted some delicious scones at a tea held for my niece's fifth birthday party, and created this copycat recipe. We love them! I take the scones to share at work and my co-workers think they're great too.

3 c. all-purpose flour
1/2 c. sugar
1 T. baking powder
1/2 t. baking soda
1/2 t. salt
3/4 c. butter
1 c. orange-flavored sweetened
    dried cranberries

1/2 c. chopped walnuts
2 T. orange zest
1 c. buttermilk
1/2 c. milk
1 egg, beaten
Optional: butter, jam

In a large bowl, combine flour, sugar, baking powder, baking soda and salt. Stir well to blend. Cut in butter with your fingers or a pastry blender until mixture resembles coarse crumbs. Add cranberries, walnuts and orange zest. Add buttermilk; stir with a fork until just moistened. On a sugared or floured surface, roll or pat dough out into a 7-1/2 inch circle. Cut into 12 wedges. If preferred, form dough by hand into 12 rounded scones. Place scones on greased baking sheets, 2 inches apart. Whisk together milk and egg; brush mixture over scones. Bake at 400 degrees for 15 minutes, or until lightly golden. Serve warm with butter and jam, if desired. Makes one dozen.

Not sure if that can of baking powder in the pantry is still good? Try this simple test: stir one teaspoon baking powder into 1/2 cup hot water. If it fizzes, go ahead and use it...if not, toss it out.

Cinnamon Sensation Bread

Janis Parr
Campbellford, Ontario

This is a delicious breakfast bread, rich, spicy and oh-so good!

2 T. butter, softened
1-1/2 c. sugar
1 egg, beaten
2 c. all-purpose flour

2 t. baking powder
1/4 t. salt
1 c. milk

In a large bowl, blend butter and sugar; stir in egg. Add flour, baking powder and salt alternately with milk; mix well. Pour batter into a greased 8"x8" baking pan; sprinkle with Cinnamon Topping. Bake at 375 degrees for 30 to 35 minutes, until a toothpick inserted in the center tests clean. Cut into squares; serve warm. Makes 6 servings.

Cinnamon Topping:

1 c. brown sugar, packed
1/4 c. butter, softened

3/4 t. cinnamon

In a bowl, work together butter and brown sugar with your fingertips until well mixed. Stir in cinnamon.

To accurately measure flour, first use a spoon to fluff up the flour while it's still in the container. Then, spoon flour into the measuring cup and level with a knife.

Ready-in-an-Hour Bread

Cindy Neel
Gooseberry Patch

Use this dough to make cinnamon rolls too.

3 to 4 c. all-purpose flour,
　　divided
1 env. active dry yeast
1 T. sugar
1 t. salt

1/2 c. water
1/3 c. milk
1 T. butter
2 eggs, divided

In a large bowl, combine 1-1/2 cups flour, yeast, sugar and salt; set aside. Heat water, milk and butter in a saucepan over medium-low heat, stirring occasionally, for 5 minutes; do not boil. Remove from heat and stir into flour mixture. Add one egg, stirring to combine. Add enough of remaining flour to make dough easy to handle, but not too stiff. On a lightly floured surface, knead dough about 5 minutes, until smooth and springy. Form into a loaf. Place on a lightly greased baking sheet. Cover with a tea towel and let rise in a warm place for 30 minutes. Beat remaining egg; brush over entire loaf. Bake at 400 degrees for 15 to 20 minutes, until golden. Makes one loaf.

Variation:

Cinnamon Rolls: Prepare dough; knead on a floured surface. Roll out dough into a round, 1/4-inch thick. Brush generously with melted butter. Mix 1/2 cup sugar and 2 teaspoons cinnamon; sprinkle over dough. Roll up dough; slice 3/4-inch thick. Put slices into a greased 13"x9" baking pan. Cover with a tea towel; let rise for 30 minutes. Bake at 400 degrees for 15 to 18 minutes, until golden. Drizzle with powdered sugar icing; sprinkle with chopped pecans, if desired. Makes 8 to 12 rolls.

Need some softened butter in a hurry? Grate chilled sticks of butter with a cheese grater...it will soften in just minutes.

Mel's Cloverleaf Rolls

Melody Meadows
Saint Albans, WV

Mmm...hot homemade rolls for dinner! We always serve these yeast rolls on special occasions and everyone just loves them.

2 c. warm water
2 envs. active dry yeast
1/2 c. sugar
1/2 c. oil
6 to 8 c. all-purpose flour, divided

Heat water until very warm, about 110 to 115 degrees. In a large bowl, mix water and yeast; stir until yeast is dissolved. Add sugar and oil; stir until sugar is dissolved. Stir in 6 cups flour. Stir in enough of remaining flour until dough is no longer sticky. Cover with a tea towel. Let rise in a warm place until double in bulk, one to 1-1/2 hours. Grease 2 muffin tins. Form dough into 1-1/2 inch balls; place 3 balls in each muffin cup. Let rise again until double. Bake at 450 degrees for 15 to 20 minutes, until lightly golden. Makes 2 dozen.

Grandma's Crescent Rolls

Sue Neely
Greenville, IL

These dinner rolls are one of my grandma's recipes that I love. Whenever I smell them baking, it brings back wonderful memories.

1/3 c. water
1 env. active dry yeast
1 c. milk
1 egg, beaten
1/3 to 1/2 c. sugar
1 t. salt
3/4 c. shortening, melted
4 c. all-purpose flour

Heat water until very warm, about 110 to 115 degrees. Dissolve yeast in water; set aside. In a large bowl, mix together milk, egg, sugar, salt and shortening. Stir in yeast mixture. Cover with a tea towel; let rise in a warm place for 2 hours. On a floured surface, roll out dough into an 8-inch circle. Cut into 8 wedges. Roll up wedges, starting at the large end. Place on greased baking sheets; let rise for about 30 minutes. Bake at 400 degrees for 15 to 20 minutes, until golden. Makes 8 rolls.

Our Daily Bread

Tricia Millix
Willington, CT

With nine children in our farmhouse, my father baked a lot of bread! We loved to watch him mix the dough and waited for it to be finished. It was an all-day process, so when he started making this easier version of his bread, we were fortunate to be able to enjoy more of it and with less impatience! It's still a staple at my house.

2 c. water	2 T. oil
2 T. active dry yeast	1 t. salt
1/4 c. sugar	4 to 5 c. all-purpose flour

Heat water until very warm, about 110 to 115 degrees. In the bowl of an electric stand mixer, combine water, yeast and sugar. Stir until sugar dissolves; let stand for 10 minutes. Add oil and salt. Stir in flour, one cup at a time, until dough forms and comes off the side of the bowl. Slowly start mixer; beat with dough hook on medium speed for 5 minutes. Place dough on a lightly floured surface; divide into 2 parts. Place in 2 greased 9"x5" loaf pans. Cover with tea towels and let rise in a warm place for 30 minutes. Bake at 400 degrees for 15 minutes, or until tops are golden. Turn loaves out of pans onto a wire rack; let cool. Makes 2 loaves.

Talk of joy: there may be things better
than beef stew and baked potatoes and
homemade bread...there may be.

– David Grayson

Garlic-Cheddar Beer Biscuits

Amanda Kisting
Dubuque, IA

*My family loves the arrival of fall, when these cake-like biscuits
reappear on our table. They're perfect with any cold-weather dish...
the aroma of the garlic warms the whole house as they bake.*

1/4 c. butter, sliced
6 cloves garlic, minced
2-1/2 c. self-rising flour
2 T. sugar
12-oz. bottle regular or
   non-alcoholic beer, room
   temperature

3/4 c. shredded sharp Cheddar
   cheese
1/4 t. Italian seasoning

Combine butter and garlic in a microwave-safe dish. Microwave until
butter is melted, 30 seconds to one minute. In a large bowl, combine
remaining ingredients and garlic mixture. Stir until moistened. Spray a
12-cup muffin tin with non-stick vegetable spray. Divide batter evenly
among muffin cups. Bake at 400 degrees for 15 minutes, or until tops
just begin to turn golden. Immediately turn biscuits out onto a plate
and serve. Makes one dozen.

No self-rising flour in the pantry? Try this! To equal one cup self-rising
flour, substitute one cup all-purpose flour plus 1-1/2 teaspoons
baking powder and 1/2 teaspoon salt.

Onion & Dill Yeast Bread

Mandy Bird
Holbrook, ID

My mother-in-law Irene is the best breadmaker that I know.
I can't get enough of her bread! It is so light and fluffy that
one slice is never enough.

1/4 c. warm water
1 env. active dry yeast
1 c. small-curd cottage cheese
2 T. sugar
2 T. dried minced onion
2 t. dill weed
1 t. salt

1/4 t. baking soda
1 T. butter, softened
1 egg
2-1/4 to 2-1/2 c. all-purpose
  flour
Garnish: melted butter

Heat water until very warm, about 110 to 115 degrees. Put yeast in a large bowl and add water; set aside for 10 minutes. Meanwhile, warm cottage cheese in a small saucepan over low heat. To yeast mixture in bowl, add cottage cheese and remaining ingredients except flour and garnish. Stir to combine. Add enough flour to make a stiff dough; mix well. Cover with a tea towel and let rise in a warm place until double in bulk, about 2 hours. Stir down dough; transfer to a greased 9"x5" loaf pan. Let rise again until double in bulk, about 2 hours. Bake at 350 degrees for 40 to 50 minutes, until golden. Remove from oven; immediately brush the top with butter. Makes one loaf.

Ovens may vary, so set a kitchen timer when the pan goes into the oven. Check for doneness after the shortest baking time given... if a little more time is needed, be sure to watch carefully.

Becki's French Bread

Becki Etling
Blairsville, PA

My favorite bread recipe! It's light and delicious...perfect for serving with a favorite meal or for making sandwiches.

1-1/2 c. warm water, divided
1 env. active dry yeast
1 T. sugar

1-1/2 t. salt
2 T. oil
4 c. all-purpose flour

Heat water until very warm, about 110 to 115 degrees. In a large bowl, dissolve yeast in 1/2 cup warm water. Add sugar and salt; let stand until bubbly, about 5 minutes. Add oil and remaining warm water; mix well. Add flour, one cup at a time, mixing well after each addition. Let rise 10 minutes in a warm place, kneading dough down 4 times every 5 minutes. Divide dough into 2 balls; let rise in a warm place for 15 minutes. On a lightly floured surface, roll out each ball into a 15-inch by 12-inch rectangle. Starting on one long edge, roll up each rectangle lengthwise, tucking in ends as you roll. Place each loaf on a lightly greased baking sheet, seam-side down. With a serrated knife, make shallow cuts across loaves every 2 inches. Cover and let rise again for 1-1/2 hours. Bake at 350 degrees for 30 to 35 minutes, until golden. Makes 2 loaves.

Make the most of leftover slices of home-baked bread...turn them into crispy croutons for soups and salads. Toss bread cubes with olive oil and chopped herbs. Toast on a baking sheet at 400 degrees for 5 to 10 minutes, until golden.

Irish Soda Bread

Helen Adams
Enchanted Oaks, TX

I make this rustic bread in my Irish grandmother's cast-iron skillet. It brings back so many memories of our wonderful Irish dinners together.

4 c. all-purpose flour
1/4 c. sugar
1-1/2 t. baking soda
1-1/2 t. cream of tartar

1-1/2 t. salt
2 T. butter, softened
1-1/2 c. buttermilk

In a large bowl, mix flour, sugar, baking soda, cream of tartar and salt. Blend in butter until fully mixed. Make a well in the center. Pour in buttermilk; gradually stir in buttermilk until well mixed. Turn out dough onto a floured surface; knead until a sticky dough forms. Place dough ball in a well-oiled cast-iron skillet. With a serrated knife, score an X in top of dough. Bake at 400 degrees for 25 minutes. Cover with aluminum foil; return to oven for 15 minutes. Immediately turn loaf out of skillet; serve warm. Makes one loaf.

Tuck a crock of honey butter into a basket alongside a loaf of fresh-baked bread...what a scrumptious way to tell a friend, "I'm thinking of you."

Honey-Do Biscuits

Rogina Pyron
Irving, TX

Whenever my hubby Dennis does something awesome or I need him to do something for me, I make these biscuits for him for breakfast or dinner. He loves them! He always wants these when I bake a ham and make red-eye gravy...he calls them great sopping biscuits.

2 c. warm water
2 envs. active dry yeast
1/4 c. sugar
5 c. all-purpose flour, divided
1/2 c. powdered dry milk

1-1/2 t. baking powder
1-1/2 t. salt
1/2 c. chilled butter
Garnish: melted butter

Heat water until very warm, about 110 to 115 degrees. In a bowl, combine warm water, yeast and sugar; set aside for 5 minutes. In a separate large bowl, stir together one cup flour, powdered milk, baking powder and salt. Cut in butter with 2 forks until pea-size lumps form. Add yeast mixture and mix thoroughly. Add remaining flour, a little at a time, until a sticky dough forms. Turn out dough onto a floured surface; knead 15 to 20 times. Roll out 1/2-inch thick; cut out biscuits with a round biscuit cutter. Place biscuits on a greased baking sheet; brush tops with melted butter. Let rise for about 40 minutes. Bake at 450 degrees for 10 to 12 minutes, until golden. Remove from oven; brush tops again with melted butter. Serve warm or cold; may be reheated in the microwave for a few seconds. Makes about one dozen.

Keep shopping simple...make a shopping list that includes all the ingredients you use often, plus a few blank lines for special items.

Best-Ever Refrigerator Rolls

Patty Fosnight
Wildorado, TX

These rolls always turn out wonderful! It's a convenient recipe since the dough can be stirred up whenever you have a few minutes, then tucked in the fridge to bake later.

1 c. warm water
2 envs. active dry yeast
1/2 c. butter, melted and slightly
    cooled
1/2 c. sugar

3 eggs, beaten
1 t. salt
4 to 4-1/2 c. all-purpose flour
Optional: additional melted
    butter

Heat water until very warm, about 110 to 115 degrees. In a large bowl, combine warm water and yeast. Let stand until foamy, 5 to 10 minutes. Stir in butter, sugar, eggs and salt. Beat in flour, one cup at a time, until dough is too stiff to mix. Cover with a tea towel; refrigerate for 2 hours to 4 days. Turn chilled dough out onto a lightly floured board. Divide dough into 24 equal pieces; roll each into a smooth ball. Place balls in even rows in a greased 13"x9" baking pan. Cover and let rise again until double, about one hour. Bake at 375 degrees for 15 to 20 minutes, until rolls are golden. Brush warm rolls with melted butter, if desired. Makes 2 dozen.

A pat of scrumptious herb butter makes fresh-baked rolls taste even better. Blend 1/2 cup softened butter with a teaspoon each of chopped fresh parsley, dill and chives. Roll into a log or pack into a crock.

Apricot Quick Bread

Jennifer Niemi
Meadowvale, Nova Scotia

Quick breads are one of the easiest ways I know to satisfy a sweet tooth! For bake sales, I usually double this recipe and make three smaller loaves. At our latest bake sale for a local animal shelter, we raised over a thousand dollars!

2 c. all-purpose flour	1 c. dried apricots, chopped
1 c. sugar	zest of 1 orange
2 t. baking powder	1 egg
1/2 t. baking soda	1/2 c. milk
1/2 t. salt	1/2 c. orange juice
1/2 t. cinnamon	1 t. almond extract

In a large bowl, stir together flour, sugar, baking powder, baking soda and salt. Mix in cinnamon, apricots and orange zest; set aside. In a smaller bowl, whisk together remaining ingredients. Add egg mixture to flour mixture, stirring just until moistened. Spoon batter into a greased and floured 9"x4" loaf pan. Bake at 350 degrees for 55 minutes, or until a toothpick tests clean. For the most flavorful, moist bread, cool completely, wrap tightly and refrigerate for a day before serving. Makes one loaf.

Variations:

Apple Quick Bread: Omit apricots and orange zest; add one cup apples, peeled, cored and diced. Increase cinnamon to 2 teaspoons; add 1/2 teaspoon nutmeg and 1/4 teaspoon ground cloves.

Cherry Quick Bread: Decrease sugar to 3/4 cup. Omit apricots; add one cup halved maraschino cherries. Add 1/4 cup maraschino cherry juice along with orange juice.

Chocolate-Walnut Quick Bread: Omit apricots and orange zest; add 6 tablespoons plus 2-1/4 teaspoons baking cocoa and 1-1/4 cups toasted chopped walnuts. Use vanilla extract instead of almond.

Yummy Zucchini Oat Bread

Carrie Fostor
Baltic, OH

I tried this recipe because I wanted something a little different, and it's a winner. Everyone loves this bread...my little boys think it's the best ever! Wrapped loaves makes nice gifts too.

2 c. zucchini, grated
2 c. all-purpose flour
1 c. quick-cooking oats,
   uncooked
1-1/2 c. sugar
1 c. canola oil
3 eggs

2 t. vanilla extract
1 t. baking powder
1 t. baking soda
1-1/2 t. cinnamon
Optional: semi-sweet chocolate
   chips, raisins or chopped
   walnuts

Combine all ingredients except optional ones in a large bowl. Beat with an electric mixer on medium speed until moistened. Stir in optional ingredients, if desired. Divide batter between two greased and floured 8"x"4 loaf pans. Bake at 325 degrees for 60 to 70 minutes, until a toothpick inserted in the center tests clean. May also use 2 greased and floured 12-cup muffin tins; fill cups 2/3 full and bake at 325 degrees for 25 to 30 minutes. Baked loaves or muffins freeze well. Makes 2 loaves or 2 dozen muffins.

Whip up a tasty cinnamon glaze to drizzle over your favorite quick bread. Mix 1/2 cup powdered sugar and 1/4 teaspoon cinnamon. Add one teaspoon light corn syrup; stir in apple juice, one tablespoon at a time, until a drizzling consistency is reached.

Best-Ever Buttermilk Cornbread

Stephanie Collins
Martinsburg, WV

My mother's mother's favorite, must-have-with-chili cornbread.
She was very frugal and this helped balance a thrifty meal.
The cast-iron skillet is a must!

2 T. bacon drippings
1 c. yellow cornmeal
1 T. all-purpose flour
1-1/2 t. baking powder
1/4 t. baking soda
1/4 t. salt

1 c. buttermilk
1 egg
Optional: 2 to 3 ears sweet corn,
   kernels sliced off
Garnish: butter

In an 8" cast-iron skillet, heat bacon drippings in a 450-degree oven.
Coat sides of skillet with melted drippings; return skillet to oven to
preheat. In a bowl, combine cornmeal, flour, baking powder, baking
soda and salt. Mix well; make a well in the center. In a separate bowl,
stir together buttermilk, egg and corn, if using. Add to cornmeal
mixture, stirring just until moistened. Let batter stand for 5 minutes;
pour into hot skillet. Bake at 450 degrees for 20 minutes, or until
golden. Cut into wedges; serve warm with butter. Makes 8 servings.

Most quick bread and biscuit recipes call for one cup of buttermilk or less.
If you don't want to buy a whole quart, you can replace it with soured
milk. Simply add one tablespoon of white vinegar or lemon juice to
one cup of whole milk and let stand for five minutes.

Cheddar Corn Muffins

Mariann Raftery
New Rochelle, NY

I bake these muffins to share with anyone who's sick or in need of cheering...they're very comforting.

1-1/2 c. all-purpose flour
1-1/8 c. cornmeal
3/4 c. sugar
3/4 t. baking soda
1-1/2 c. sour cream

2 eggs, beaten
3/4 c. butter, melted and slightly cooled
1-1/2 c. shredded Cheddar cheese

In a large bowl, mix together flour, cornmeal, sugar and baking soda. Add sour cream, eggs and melted butter. Stir with a wooden spoon until mixed well. Add cheese; mix again. Spoon batter into paper-lined muffin cups, filling 2/3 full. Bake at 375 degrees for 20 to 25 minutes, until lightly golden. Serve warm or cooled. Muffins freeze well. Makes about 1-1/2 dozen.

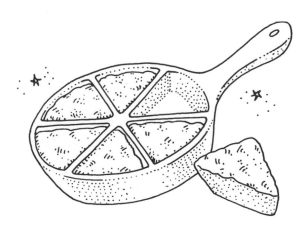

For cornbread with a crisp, golden crust, bake it in a vintage sectioned cast-iron skillet.

Country Biscuits 5 Ways

Robin Hill
Rochester, NY

*Back in the 60s when I was first learning to bake, my mom gave me
this recipe that she'd found in a flour company's pamphlet.*

2 c. self-rising flour   2/3 c. milk
1/4 c. shortening

Place flour in a bowl. With 2 knives, cut in shortening until mixture
is like coarse crumbs. Gradually stir in milk until a soft dough forms.
Turn out dough onto a floured surface; knead gently for 6 to 8 strokes.
Lightly roll or pat out to 1/2-inch thickness. Cut out biscuits with a
floured cutter. Place on an ungreased baking sheet. Bake at 450 degrees
for 12 to 15 minutes, until golden. Makes about one dozen.

Variations:

Buttermilk Biscuits: Add 1/4 teaspoon baking soda to flour mixture;
use buttermilk instead of milk.

Cheese Biscuits: Add one cup shredded sharp Cheddar cheese to flour
mixture before adding milk.

Onion Biscuits: Add one tablespoon dried, minced onion to flour
mixture before adding milk.

Bacon Biscuits: Add 4 slices crisply cooked and crumbled bacon to
flour mixture before adding milk.

Don't have a biscuit cutter handy? Use the open end of a clean,
empty soup can to cut biscuit dough.

Cool Refreshing SALADS

Herbed Cherry Tomatoes

Debbie Privett
Tacoma, WA

This is a recipe my mom got from her own mother. My family can't wait to make it each summer! We enjoy these tomatoes served over a scoop of cottage cheese.

2 c. cherry tomatoes, sliced
1/4 c. oil
3 T. red wine vinegar
1/4 c. fresh parsley, snipped

1/2 t. dried basil
1/2 t. dried oregano
1/2 t. salt
1/2 t. sugar

Place tomatoes in a serving bowl; set aside. In a separate bowl, whisk together remaining ingredients. Drizzle oil mixture over tomatoes and mix well. For the best flavor, cover and refrigerate up to 24 hours before serving. Serves 4.

Fresh-picked tomatoes will keep their sun-ripened flavor best
if stored on the counter until used.

Sour Cream Cucumber Salad

Jenn Vallimont
Kersey, PA

We look forward to using fresh cucumbers and onions from our garden. My mom has been making this salad for years, and it has become a favorite for my family as well.

3 c. cucumbers, peeled if desired
    and sliced
1/2 c. onion, coarsely chopped
1/2 c. sour cream

1/4 c. oil
2 T. sugar
1 T. vinegar
salt to taste

Toss together cucumbers and onion in a serving bowl; set aside. Combine remaining ingredients in a small bowl; mix well. Pour sour cream mixture over vegetables and toss to coat. Cover and refrigerate for several hours to overnight. Mix well before serving. Serves 4.

Onions are delicious in salads. If a milder flavor is preferred, cover sliced onions with cold water and a splash of vinegar for half an hour. Drain and add to salad.

Leona's Old-Time Potato Salad

Pat Beach
Fisherville, KY

*My brother-in-law's mother was a wonderful cook who
specialized in down-home cooking. Her potato salad
still gets me rave reviews every time I serve it.*

7 to 8 redskin potatoes
2 stalks celery, chopped
1 onion, chopped
1 c. pickle relish
1 c. mayonnaise or mayonnaise-
   type salad dressing

1/4 c. mustard
5 eggs, hard-boiled, peeled
   and chopped
1 t. salt
1/2 t. pepper

In a large saucepan, cover unpeeled potatoes with cold water. Bring to
a boil over medium-high heat. Cook for 15 to 20 minutes, until fork-
tender. Drain and let cool. In a large bowl, combine celery, onion and
relish; mix well. Add remaining ingredients; set aside. Peel potatoes;
cut into quarters lengthwise and slice. Add to celery mixture; stir well.
Cover and refrigerate until serving time. Makes 8 to 10 servings.

Try this simple way to make hard-boiled eggs. Cover eggs with
an inch of water in a saucepan and place over medium-high heat.
As soon as the water comes to a boil, cover the pan and remove
from heat. Let stand for 18 to 20 minutes...cover with
ice water, peel and they're done.

Tangy Tomato-Broccoli Salad

Teri Lindquist
Gurnee, IL

This recipe started out very simply as fresh broccoli with a tangy dressing. For Christmas, I added grape tomatoes to make it red & green. Then last summer, I added the bacon and served it for lunch with buttered biscuits and ice tea. I enjoy creating recipes, and am pleased this turned out to be a family favorite!

3 lbs. broccoli, cut into bite-size
   flowerets
1 pt. grape tomatoes

3 slices bacon, crisply cooked
   and crumbled
coarse pepper to taste

In a large clear glass serving bowl, mix together broccoli, tomatoes and bacon. Drizzle Dijon Dressing over salad and toss gently. Season with pepper. Cover and refrigerate one to 2 hours, stirring several times while chilling. Makes 6 servings.

Dijon Dressing:

1/3 c. extra-virgin olive oil
1/4 c. cider vinegar
3 T. light brown sugar, packed

1 T. Dijon mustard
2 cloves garlic, minced
1/2 t. salt

In a small bowl, whisk together all ingredients.

Avoid soggy salads...simply pour salad dressing in the bottom of your salad bowl, then add greens on top. Toss just before serving.

Bob's Nana's Mexican Salad

Cathie Lopez
La Mirada, CA

A yummy quick salad that's a meal in itself! This recipe was passed down by an old friend. Browned ground beef or ground turkey can easily be added, if an even heartier salad is desired.

1 head lettuce, shredded
3 tomatoes, chopped
2 avocados, halved, pitted
   and sliced
Optional: 4-oz. can sliced black
   olives, drained

2 15-oz. cans ranch-style
   beans, drained
1 c. shredded Cheddar cheese
Catalina salad dressing to taste
10-1/4 oz. pkg. corn chips

In a large bowl, combine lettuce, vegetables, beans and cheese; toss to mix. Cover and chill. At serving time, drizzle with dressing; add corn chips and toss to mix. Serves 6.

Serve Bob's Nana's Mexican Salad in tortilla bowls. Lightly brush corn tortillas on both sides with olive oil. Carefully press into oven-safe soup bowls, folding up the edges. Bake at 325 degrees for 8 to 10 minutes, until crispy and golden.

Summer Corn Salad

Cris Goode
Mooresville, IN

We love this salad for summer dinners and fuss over the leftovers the next day! It goes perfectly with anything from the grill.

4 ears sweet corn, or 10-oz. pkg.
   frozen corn
1 avocado, halved, pitted and
   chopped
4 tomatoes, chopped
1/4 c. fresh basil, chopped
4 cloves garlic, minced
juice of 2 limes

If using ears of corn, cover them with water in a large saucepan; cook over medium-high heat until tender, 8 to 10 minutes. Drain; cool and slice off kernels. If using frozen corn, cook according to package directions; cool. In a large bowl, combine corn and remaining ingredients. Mix gently and serve immediately. Serves 6 to 8.

Garden-Fresh Spicy Tomato Salad

Linda Brown
Lone Tree, CO

Just the recipe to make when you have too many fresh tomatoes or simply want a different salad for a change. Cool and refreshing with a lively kick!

3 tomatoes, chopped
1/2 c. red onion, chopped
1 cucumber, chopped
1 T. red pepper flakes
1/4 c. rice wine vinegar

Place vegetables in a glass serving bowl. Add pepper flakes and vinegar; toss to mix well. Cover and chill. Stir just before serving. Makes 4 servings.

Spoon fruit or veggie salads into mini Mason jars...fun for a summer buffet and convenient to tuck in a picnic basket.

Kathie's Creamy Coleslaw

*Kathie Poritz-Craig
Burlington, WI*

My friend Chuck always asked me to make my coleslaw for his workplace's potlucks & picnics. His co-workers much preferred it to the soggy store-bought kind. It's a hit at home too. This recipe can easily be doubled or tripled for a large gathering.

3 c. cabbage, coarsely chopped
   or shredded
1/3 c. green pepper, chopped
1/3 c. onion, chopped
1/2 c. mayonnaise or
   mayonnaise-style salad
   dressing

1 T. sugar
1 T. vinegar
1/2 t. salt
1/2 t. celery seed

Combine cabbage, green pepper and onion in a large serving bowl. In a separate bowl, blend together remaining ingredients. Drizzle mayonnaise mixture over vegetables; toss. Cover and chill until serving time. Makes 6 to 8 servings.

When it's just too hot to cook, invite friends and neighbors over for a salad potluck. You set up a table in a shady spot and set out pitchers of ice tea...everyone brings along their favorite salad to share.

Warm Bacon-Potato Salad

Anne Alesauskas
Minocqua, WI

If you like warm German potato salad but a milder vinegar taste, you'll like this adaptation. I've eaten it after several days in the fridge...the flavor gets even better with age.

2-1/2 lbs. redskin potatoes,
    cut into 1-inch cubes
1 t. salt
6 slices bacon, chopped
1 onion, diced

2 cloves garlic, chopped
pepper to taste
5 to 6 T. fresh dill, chopped
    and divided
salt to taste

Cover potatoes with cold water in a large saucepan; add salt. Bring to a boil over high heat. Reduce heat to medium and cook for 20 minutes, or until fork-tender. Drain; place potatoes in a large bowl. Cover and keep warm. Meanwhile, in a skillet over medium heat, cook bacon until crisp. Remove bacon to a paper towel-lined plate, reserving drippings in skillet. Add onion, garlic and pepper to drippings; cook until tender, about 3 minutes. Add Mustard Vinaigrette to onion mixture. Cook until thickened and reduced, stirring occasionally, about 3 minutes. Add potatoes, bacon and 4 tablespoons dill to skillet; toss to coat. Cook for 3 minutes. Season with salt and more pepper. Garnish with remaining dill; serve warm. Makes 8 servings.

Mustard Vinaigrette:

1 c. white vinegar
1 T. coarse-grained mustard

1 T. sugar

Stir together ingredients in a small bowl.

Cloth napkins are so much nicer than paper ones, so why not whip up some fun napkin rings for them? Stitch a big vintage button or a pretty silk flower onto colorful new hair elastics. Done in a snap!

Simple Asparagus Salad

*Lisa Ann Panzino-DiNunzio
Vineland, NJ*

A simple way to use fresh asparagus that tastes so good!

1 bunch asparagus, ends
    trimmed
juice of 2 lemons

1/4 c. extra-virgin olive oil
2 T. cider vinegar
sea salt and pepper to taste

In a steamer basket, steam asparagus over boiling water until fork-tender, 3 to 5 minutes. Drain asparagus and pat dry. Place in a serving dish; cover and chill completely. Just before serving, whisk together remaining ingredients in a small bowl; drizzle over asparagus. Serves 4.

Chilled Green Bean Salad

*Jen Thomas
Santa Rosa, CA*

*Crisp-tender green beans dressed with lime juice are
a flavorful change from long-simmered beans.*

3/4 lb. green beans, trimmed
2 T. water
4 green onions, sliced
2 stalks celery, chopped

1/3 c. fresh parsley, snipped
2 T. olive oil
2 T. lime juice
salt and pepper

Add green beans and water to a microwave-safe dish. Cover and microwave for 5 minutes, stirring after 3 minutes. Drain; rinse with cold water and drain again. Transfer to a serving dish. Add remaining ingredients; toss. Cover; let stand at room temperature for up to 30 minutes before serving. Serves 4.

It's not how much we have, but how much
we enjoy, that makes happiness.
    —Charles Haddon-Spurgeon

Rainbow Rotini Salad

Zoe Bennett
Columbia, SC

Perfect for picnics! Make it the night before and pack it to go.

12-oz. pkg. rainbow rotini pasta,
  uncooked
1/2 c. green pepper, chopped
1/2 c. red pepper, chopped
1/2 c. red onion, chopped
1/2 c. celery, chopped

1/2 c. carrot, peeled and cut
  into very thin strips
1/2 c. sliced black olives,
  drained
1/4 lb. Cheddar cheese, diced
1 c. ranch salad dressing

Cook pasta according to package directions; drain and rinse with cold water. Place pasta in a large serving bowl; add vegetables and cheese. Drizzle with salad dressing; toss well. Cover and chill 8 hours to overnight. Serves 8.

Variation:

Pizza Pasta Salad: Use plain rotini instead of rainbow. Omit celery and carrot; add 1/2 cup each diced tomatoes and diced pepperoni. Use mozzarella cheese and tomato & bacon salad dressing. Garnish with grated Parmesan cheese and a sprinkle of dried oregano.

Carrying a salad to a school potluck or a family picnic? Mix it up
in a plastic zipping bag instead of a bowl, seal and set it on ice
in a picnic cooler. No more worries about leaks or spills!

Gingered Chicken & Fruit Salad

Beverley Williams
San Antonio, TX

This is a great summertime salad! It is refreshing, fast to make and doesn't heat up your kitchen. Omit the chicken for a delicious fruit salad. May be served in lettuce-lined pita pockets.

1-1/2 to 2 c. mayonnaise
2 T. ground ginger
2 c. cooked chicken breast, cubed
1 c. green and/or red seedless grapes, halved lengthwise

3 Red Delicious apples, peeled, cored and diced
3 Granny Smith apples, peeled, cored and diced
1 c. pineapple chunks
1/2 c. slivered almonds

In a small bowl, stir together mayonnaise and ginger; set aside. Combine remaining ingredients in a large bowl. Add mayonnaise mixture; toss lightly until well blended and coated. Cover and chill until serving time. Makes 8 servings.

Hawaiian Salad

Sharry Murawski
Oak Forest, IL

Whenever I need a quick side dish, this is one of my go-to recipes. I usually have everything in the pantry...it's ready in just minutes!

1 c. pineapple chunks
11-oz. can mandarin oranges, drained
1/2 c. sour cream

1 c. mini marshmallows
2 T. sweetened flaked coconut, toasted

Combine pineapple and oranges in a bowl. Gently stir in sour cream. Fold in marshmallows and coconut. Refrigerate until ready to serve. Serves 4.

To toast coconut, place in a dry skillet and heat over medium-low heat. Cook and stir until lightly toasted, about 3 minutes.

Strawberry-Bacon Spinach Salad

Kathy Harris
Council Grove, KS

This is my utility salad, as I like to call it! Whenever I need a simple fresh salad, I always rely on this one as the ingredients are available year 'round and everyone loves it. I have even served it at Thanksgiving...a welcome addition to an otherwise heavy meal.

8 slices bacon
6-oz. pkg. fresh baby spinach
1 pt. strawberries, hulled and
    sliced
1/4 c. red onion, chopped

1/4 c. chopped walnuts
1 c. mayonnaise
1/2 c. sugar
1/4 c. raspberry vinegar

In a skillet over medium heat, cook bacon until crisp. Drain on a paper towel-lined plate; cool and crumble. In a salad bowl, combine spinach, strawberries, bacon, onion and walnuts. In a small bowl or pitcher, combine mayonnaise, sugar and vinegar; mix well. Serve dressing alongside salad, or drizzle over salad and toss just before serving. Makes 6 to 8 servings.

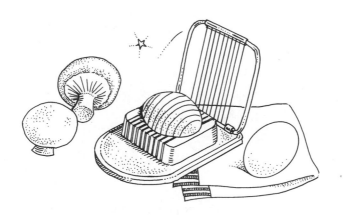

Speedy salad topper! An egg slicer makes short work of slicing mushrooms and olives as well as hard-boiled eggs. It can turn out uniform slices of soft fruit like strawberries and bananas too.

Garden Macaroni Salad

Ellie Brandel
Clackamas, OR

What a delicious way to get your vegetables! All the veggies are readily available year 'round too.

8-oz. pkg. elbow macaroni, uncooked
3/4 c. mayonnaise
1 t. salt
1/4 t. dried basil
2 tomatoes, diced

1 c. cucumber, diced
1 c. celery, sliced
1/4 c. green pepper, diced
1/4 c. radishes, sliced
2 T. green onions, sliced

Cook macaroni according to package directions; drain and rinse with cold water. In a large serving bowl, stir together mayonnaise, salt and basil. Add macaroni and remaining ingredients; stir to coat. Cover and chill until serving time. Makes 8 servings.

Serve up a do-it-yourself salad bar on busy nights. Alongside a large bowl of crisp greens, set out muffin tins filled with chopped veggies, diced hard-boiled egg, grilled sliced chicken, shredded cheese and creamy dressings. A basket of hot rolls and a pitcher of icy lemonade round out the menu...dig in!

Veggie Trio Salad

Linda Myers
Denver, MO

There were gardens galore this year, and everyone had bumper crops. I've had a large amount of yellow squash, one neighbor had cherry tomatoes and yet another neighbor red onions. We all shared our harvest, and I decided to use just these three in a recipe.

2 c. cherry tomatoes, halved	2 T. balsamic vinegar
1 red onion, halved and sliced	2 T. extra-virgin olive oil
1 to 2 yellow squash, peeled and cut into 1-inch cubes	1/4 t. salt
	1/4 t. pepper

Combine vegetables in a large serving bowl and toss with a spoon. Whisk together vinegar, oil, salt and pepper. Pour over vegetables and stir well to coat. Serve immediately, or cover and chill. Serves 4 to 6.

If you bought a bunch of fresh herbs for a recipe that calls for just a couple of tablespoons, chop the extra herbs and add to a tossed salad. Fresh parsley, mint, dill, chives and basil all add zest.

Marla's Greek Salad

Marla Caldwell
Forest, IN

My family loves salads. This is one of our favorites and one I am most likely to have all the ingredients on hand most of the time. I get lots of requests for this at family gatherings too! I usually come home with an empty bowl.

1 head romaine lettuce, torn	1 green pepper, cut into rings
3/4 c. medium black olives	1/2 red onion, thinly sliced
3/4 c. sliced mushrooms	1/2 c. crumbled feta cheese

In a large salad bowl, combine all ingredients. Gradually add enough Creamy Balsamic Dressing to coat, tossing gently. Serve with remaining dressing on the side. Makes 6 to 8 servings.

Creamy Balsamic Dressing:

1 c. mayonnaise	1-1/2 t. dried oregano
1/2 c. olive oil	1 t. dried basil
1/4 c. balsamic vinegar	1/4 t. salt
1 clove garlic, minced	1/2 t. pepper

Combine all ingredients, stirring with a wire whisk.

Lacy cheese crisps are tasty with salads or just as a snack. Spoon mounds of freshly shredded Parmesan cheese, 4 inches apart, onto a baking sheet lined with parchment paper. Bake at 400 degrees for 5 to 7 minutes, until melted and golden, then cool.

Quick Tomato & Olive Salad

Krista Marshall
Fort Wayne, IN

This salad is perfect on a busy night when supper needs to be quick. It's easily adapted with any veggies, including those fresh from a farmer's market.

1 pt. cherry tomatoes, halved
1/2 c. green olives with
  pimentos, sliced
1/4 c. Kalamata olives, sliced
3 T. capers, drained

1 T. dried parsley
salt and pepper to taste
1/2 to 3/4 c. Italian salad
  dressing
Garnish: additional dried parsley

In a salad bowl, combine vegetables, parsley, salt and pepper; toss to mix. Add dressing to desired consistency. Cover and chill at least 2 hours. At serving time, garnish with parsley; use a slotted spoon to serve. Makes 4 servings.

For hearty salads in a snap, keep cans of diced tomatoes, black olives, white beans and marinated artichoke hearts in the fridge. They'll be chilled and ready to toss with fresh greens at a moment's notice.

Orchard Salad

Carrie O'Shea
Marina Del Rey, CA

We love this crunchy salad! Use a bottled salad dressing if time is short, but this dressing doesn't take long to stir up.

1 head romaine lettuce, torn
1 Gala apple, cored and thinly
  sliced
1 Bartlett pear, cored and thinly
  sliced
3/4 c. shredded Swiss cheese
3/4 c. cashews, coarsely chopped
1/2 c. sweetened dried
  cranberries

Toss together all ingredients in a large bowl. Serve drizzled with desired amount of Poppy Seed Dressing. Makes 6 to 8 servings.

Poppy Seed Dressing:

2/3 c. oil
1/2 c. sugar
1/3 c. lemon juice
1-1/2 T. poppy seed
2 t. dried, minced onion
1 t. Dijon mustard
1/2 t. salt

Combine all ingredients in a blender; cover and process until smooth. May keep refrigerated up to one week; serve at room temperature.

Sugared nuts are delicious on salads. Place 3/4 cup walnut or pecan halves, 1/4 cup sugar and one teaspoon butter in a cast-iron skillet. Cook and stir over medium heat for about 7 minutes, until sugar is golden and melted. Spread carefully on a greased baking sheet to cool.

Toni's Curried Chicken & Shells Salad

Pat Beach
Fisherville, KY

I'm so excited to share this delectable recipe with you. My daughter Toni makes it quite often for luncheons with her lady friends. We have also served it as a main dish at family birthday dinners. It is absolutely delicious. It also makes a very elegant presentation when served with a big bowl of fruit salad and crusty rolls. I hope you enjoy it as much as we do!

12-oz. pkg. medium pasta
   shells, uncooked
1 deli roast chicken
1/2 c. raisins
1/2 c. celery, diced

1/4 c. slivered almonds
salt and pepper to taste
1 c. light mayonnaise
1/2 c. mango chutney
2 t. curry powder

Cook pasta according to package directions; drain and rinse with cold water. Meanwhile, shred chicken, discarding skin and bones. Place pasta in a large serving bowl; add chicken, raisins, celery and almonds. Season with salt and pepper. In a small bowl, mix remaining ingredients. Add just enough of mayonnaise mixture to lightly coat pasta mixture. Cover and chill before serving. Makes 6 servings.

Shake up a simple vinaigrette dressing. Combine 2 tablespoons cider vinegar, 6 tablespoons olive oil and one teaspoon Dijon mustard in a small jar, twist on the lid and shake well. Add salt and pepper to taste.

Loaded Potato Salad

Arden Regnier
East Moriches, NY

Our church's bake sales, held every Saturday in July, have expanded to salads, and we each have our own version of potato salad. One day I decided to make a salad with the flavors of a loaded baked potato...it became a big hit!

4 russet potatoes, peeled
   and cubed
1 t. salt
6 to 8 thick-cut slices bacon
1/2 c. mayonnaise

1/2 c. sour cream
1/2 c. shredded Cheddar cheese
1/4 c. fresh chives, chopped
salt and pepper to taste

Cover potatoes with cold water in a large saucepan; add salt. Cook over medium-high heat until fork-tender, 15 to 20 minutes. Drain; cool slightly and place in a large bowl. Meanwhile, in a skillet over medium heat, cook bacon until crisp. Drain on a paper towel-lined plate; cool and crumble. In a small bowl, combine mayonnaise, sour cream, bacon, cheese, salt and pepper, reserving some bacon, cheese or chives for garnish, if desired. Add to potatoes; mix well. Serve immediately, or cover and chill. Serves 6 to 8.

Grandma's Waldorf Salad

Anne Alesauskas
Minocqua, WI

Whenever I make this salad, I think of my grandma and great-grandma. It was always a staple on their table, especially at Easter time. Now it brings back so many sweet memories.

2 Gala apples, cored and diced
1 Granny Smith apple, cored
   and diced
1/2 c. chopped pecans or
   walnuts

1/2 c. celery, diced
1/3 c. sweetened dried
   cranberries
1/3 c. mayonnaise

Stir together all ingredients in a large bowl. Cover and chill until serving time. Serves 6.

Mabel's 24-Hour Coleslaw

Virginia Craven
Denton, TX

My mother-in-law Mabel never considered herself a great cook, but we all disagreed. Her cooking wasn't fancy, but her food was always delicious and she could really give some wonderful parties. This recipe is so quick & easy and doubles or triples well. I have been using it for 40 years and now my daughter Holly uses it too.

1-1/2 c. cider vinegar
3/4 c. sugar
1 T. dry mustard
1 t. salt
1 c. oil

2 16-oz. pkgs. shredded
   coleslaw mix with carrots
1 red onion, halved and very
   thinly sliced

In a saucepan over medium heat, combine vinegar, sugar, mustard and salt. Bring to a boil. Cook, stirring occasionally, until sugar dissolves. Remove from heat and stir in oil. In a large serving bowl, alternate layers of coleslaw mix and onion; repeat till all used. Pour warm dressing over top; mix gently. Cover and refrigerate at least 24 hours before serving. Drain liquid before serving. Will keep up to one week in the refrigerator. Serves 12.

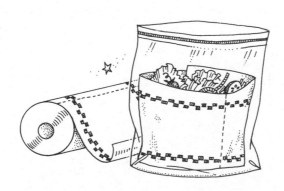

Keep leafy salad greens farmstand-fresh for up to a week. After you bring them home, rinse greens in cool water, wrap in paper towels and slip into a plastic zipping bag with several small holes cut in it. Tuck the bag in the fridge's crisper bin... ready to serve when you are!

Classic Cobb Salad

April Jacobs
Loveland, CO

*So pretty on a luncheon buffet...just add a basket of
fruit muffins and a pitcher of ice tea.*

1 head iceberg lettuce, chopped
1 c. cooked chicken breast,
  cubed
1 c. cooked ham, cubed
8 slices bacon, crisply cooked
  and crumbled
3 to 4 eggs, hard-boiled, peeled
  and sliced

1 to 2 tomatoes, cubed
1 avocado, halved, pitted and
  cubed
1/2 c. crumbled blue cheese
1/2 c. fresh parsley, chopped

Cover a large serving platter with lettuce. Arrange remaining
ingredients in rows over lettuce, one ingredient at a time. Drizzle with
Red Wine Dressing just before serving. Serves 6 to 8.

Red Wine Dressing:

1/4 c. red wine vinegar
3/4 t. salt
1/2 t. dry mustard

1/8 t. pepper
1/2 c. olive oil
1 clove garlic, pressed

In a jar with a tight-fitting lid, combine all ingredients except olive oil
and garlic. Cover jar and shake well. Add oil and garlic; cover and
shake again. Shake again just before serving.

For a new way to serve Classic Cobb Salad, layer all the
ingredients in a clear glass trifle bowl.

Perfect Peas & Pasta

Marianne Hilgenberg
Orlando, FL

My delicious pasta salad has been handed down by three generations. We call it our 3 P's Salad, and it's perfect for church luncheons, baby showers and reunions. My husband says it tastes best with BBQ chicken, ribs, burgers and hot dogs on the grill... everyone loves it! Serve it in your prettiest serving bowl.

12-oz. pkg. rotini pasta, uncooked
9-oz. pkg. frozen peas, thawed and drained
8-oz. jar sweet gherkin pickles, sliced

8-oz. pkg. sharp Cheddar cheese, diced
1 bunch green onions, sliced
12-oz. jar mayonnaise-style salad dressing

Cook pasta according to package directions, just until tender. Drain and rinse with cold water; transfer to a large serving bowl. Add remaining ingredients; top with desired amount of salad dressing. Mix gently. Cover and chill for 30 minutes to overnight before serving. Makes 12 servings.

Combine ingredients for homemade salad dressing in a squeeze bottle instead of a bowl. You can even write the ingredients on the bottle with a permanent marker. Shake the bottle to incorporate flavors and squeeze onto salad...what could be easier?

Tasty Tuna in a Tomato

Beverly Stiers
Fishers, IN

My wonderful mother was the best cook in the world! She made this tuna salad for me when I was young. I loved it then, love it now and so does my family.

2 12-oz. cans tuna, drained
5 to 6 green onions, chopped
1/2 c. celery, finely chopped
1/2 t. salt

1/4 t. pepper
bottled slaw dressing to taste
5 to 6 tomatoes
Garnish: fresh parsley sprigs

In a bowl, combine tuna, onions, celery, salt and pepper. Add salad dressing to desired consistency. Cut a very thin slice from the bottom of each tomato so it will stand upright. Cut a thin slice from the top of each tomato; scoop out pulp, creating a tomato shell. If desired, remove seeds from tomato pulp; add pulp to tuna mixture. Spoon tuna mixture into hollowed-out tomatoes. Garnish with parsley. Serves 5 to 6.

A vintage-style salad that's ready to serve in seconds! Top crisp wedges of iceberg lettuce with blue cheese salad dressing, diced tomato and bacon crumbles. Yum!

Savory Simmering SOUPS

Mom's Vegetable Beef Soup

Cindy vonHentschel
Albuquerque, NM

*My mom always made soups and chowders when the weather
got cold. This was one of my favorites...a satisfying meal
to serve up on a chilly day. Enjoy!*

2 T. oil
1 lb. stew beef cubes
1 onion, diced
3 to 4 stalks celery, sliced
3 to 4 carrots, peeled and diced
4 to 5 potatoes, peeled and
    cubed

2 c. plus 2 T. beef broth,
    divided
1 c. tomatoes, diced
2 T. all-purpose flour
salt and pepper to taste

Add oil to a large soup pot over medium-high heat. Add beef; brown
on all sides. Remove beef to a bowl and set aside. Add onion, celery
and carrots; cook until crisp-tender. Return beef to soup pot along with
potatoes and 2 cups broth. Bring to a boil over medium-high heat.
Reduce heat to medium-low. Simmer for about about 45 minutes,
stirring occasionally; add a little water, if needed. Add tomatoes;
continue to simmer for 15 minutes, or until beef is tender. Mix flour
and remaining broth in a cup; stir into stew. Cook and stir until
thickened. Season with salt and pepper. Makes 4 servings.

As an old French proverb says, to make good soup, the pot must
only simmer, or "smile." As soon as the broth comes to a boil,
turn down the heat to low. The soup will barely simmer,
with bubbles breaking very gently on the surface.

Comforting Chicken Soup

Christina Vawser
Silverado, CA

My two girls and I love this soup! Served with bread & butter and a tossed salad, it makes a quick, flavorful meal for a busy mom. Be sure to use bone-in, skin-on chicken thighs, as they add so much flavor to the soup. Cilantro maybe substituted instead of some or all of the parsley for a slightly different taste.

4 chicken thighs
2 14-1/2 oz. cans chicken broth
1 yellow onion, chopped
2 to 3 stalks celery, chopped

1 T. fresh parsley, chopped
4 green onions, chopped and
   divided

Place chicken, broth, onion, celery and parsley in a Dutch oven or soup pot. Bring to a low boil over medium heat. Reduce heat to low; cover and simmer for 20 to 30 minutes, until chicken juices run clear. Remove chicken to a plate; cool slightly. Cube chicken and return to soup; discard chicken skin and bones. Stir in most of green onions; simmer for 10 minutes more. Garnish soup bowls with remaining green onions. Serves 4.

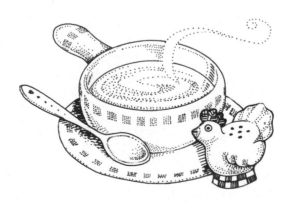

Homemade soup tastes even better if made a day ahead and refrigerated overnight. It's a snap to skim any fat too...it will solidify on the surface and can easily be scooped off.

Italian Wedding Soup

Mia Rossi
Charlotte, NC

*Serve this savory soup for lunch with warm garlic bread,
or serve smaller portions as the first course to a pasta meal.*

6 c. water
6 t. chicken bouillon granules,
  divided
1/2 lb. ground beef or turkey
1 slice bread, torn
1 egg, beaten
1 T. onion, finely chopped

2 T. carrot, peeled and grated
1/2 c. orzo or star pasta,
  uncooked
1-1/2 c. fresh spinach, shredded
1 t. dried basil
Garnish: shredded Parmesan
  cheese

In a large soup pot over medium-high heat, combine water and
5 teaspoons bouillon; bring to a boil. Meanwhile, in a bowl, combine
meat, bread, egg, onion and remaining bouillon. Form into 1/2-inch
meatballs. Add meatballs, carrot and pasta to soup pot; reduce heat
to medium and cook for 10 minutes. Stir in spinach and basil; simmer
3 to 5 minutes. Serve in \soup bowls, garnished with Parmesan cheese.
Makes 6 servings.

Make a warm loaf of crostini to serve with soup. Slice a loaf of Italian
bread into 1/2-inch slices. Brush olive oil over both sides of each slice;
sprinkle with coarse salt. Bake in a 300-degree oven for 20 minutes,
or until crisp and toasty, turning once.

Chicken & Zucchini Soup

Kay Marone
Des Moines, IA

A chicken soup that's just a little different! If I'm making it for the kids, I'll use alphabet pasta instead of the orzo just for fun.

3 14-1/2 oz. cans chicken broth
1/2 lb. boneless skinless chicken
   breast, diced
1-1/2 c. zucchini, diced
3 T. orzo pasta, uncooked
1/2 c. frozen peas

4 green onions, thinly sliced,
   white and green parts
   divided
1 T. lemon juice
1 T. fresh dill, snipped

Bring broth to a boil in a large saucepan over medium heat. Stir in chicken, zucchini and orzo; cook for 7 to 9 minutes. Stir in frozen peas and white part of onions. Reduce heat and simmer, stirring occasionally, for 3 to 5 minutes. Remove from heat; stir in lemon juice, dill and green part of onions. Serves 6.

Egg Drop Soup

Darci Heaton
Woodbury, PA

My daughter and I love egg drop soup, so we played around with different ingredients until we came up with this recipe. We love it more than our local Chinese restaurant's version!

8 c. chicken broth, divided
1 cube chicken bouillon
3 T. cornstarch

4 eggs, well beaten
Optional: wide chow mein
   noodles

Add 6-1/2 cups broth and bouillon cube to a soup pot over medium-high heat; bring to a boil. In a bowl, add cornstarch to remaining broth; stir until dissolved. Pour cornstarch mixture into boiling broth and stir. Bring broth to a rolling boil. With a fork, drizzle eggs into boiling broth; eggs should cook immediately. Simmer for one to 2 minutes. Serve topped with Chinese noodles, if desired. Serves 4 to 6.

Fireman's Beef Barley Soup

Shirley Murray
Tucson, AZ

Hearty and satisfying...real old-fashioned goodness!

2 T. oil
1 to 2 lbs. beef flank steak,
   cut into 1/2-inch cubes
1/2 c. onion, diced
3 stalks celery, diced
14-1/2 oz. can diced tomatoes
   with garlic & onion
5 c. beef broth

1 c. long-cooking pearled
   barley, uncooked
1/4 c. fresh parsley, chopped
1 T. Worcestershire sauce
3 bay leaves
1 t. fresh thyme, snipped
salt and pepper to taste

Heat oil in a large soup pot over medium-high heat; add beef. Brown beef on all sides; drain and set beef aside in a bowl. Add onion and celery to soup pot. Sauté until tender; cover and cook over medium heat for 5 minutes. Return beef to soup pot along with undrained tomatoes and remaining ingredients. Bring to a boil. Reduce heat to low; cover and simmer for 1-1/2 hours, stirring occasionally. Discard bay leaves before serving. Serves 6 to 8.

Busy day ahead? Use a slow cooker to make soup...it practically cooks itself! Soup that simmers for 2 hours on the stovetop can usually be cooked on the low setting for 6 to 8 hours or even longer.

Stuffed Pepper Soup

Kimberly Lunsford
Hill AFB, UT

The homestyle taste of stuffed peppers without all the work...
a perfect soup for a cold winter day!

2 lbs. ground beef
1/2 onion, chopped
6 c. water
8 t. beef bouillon granules
2 28-oz. cans diced tomatoes
2 c. cooked rice

1 t. paprika
2 t. salt
1/2 t. pepper
3 green, red and/or yellow
  peppers, chopped

In a large pot over medium heat, cook beef with onion until beef is no longer pink and onion is tender. Drain; add water, bouillon, tomatoes with juice, cooked rice, paprika, salt and pepper. Bring to a boil. Reduce heat to low; cover and simmer for one hour, stirring occasionally. Stir in peppers; cook, uncovered, for 10 to 15 minutes, until peppers are tender. Serves 8.

A casual potluck soup supper is perfect for catching up with family & friends. Everyone is sure to discover new favorites, so be sure to have each person bring along extra copies of his or her recipe to share.

Cowboy Soup

Marian Forck
Chamois, MO

*A longtime family favorite...I have ten brothers & sisters and
we all love this soup! We've eaten it for several days in a row
and never get tired of it, but leftovers do freeze well.*

1 to 2 lbs. ground beef
5.6-oz. pkg. Spanish rice
   mix, uncooked
1 onion, chopped
4 to 5 c. beef broth

15-oz. can mixed vegetables
14-1/2 oz. can diced tomatoes
10-oz. can diced tomatoes and
   green chiles
11-oz. can corn

In a soup pot over medium heat, brown beef with onion; drain.
Meanwhile, prepare rice according to package directions. To beef
mixture in soup pot, add cooked rice, 4 cups broth and undrained
vegetables. Bring to a boil; reduce heat to low. Simmer for about
30 minutes, adding remaining broth if a thinner consistency is desired.
Makes 8 to 10 servings.

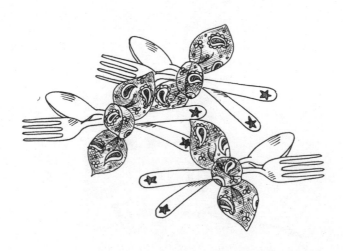

Give tonight's table a little flair...knot a cheery bandanna around
each set of flatware. Bandannas come in so many bright colors,
everyone can choose their own favorite.

Snowy-Day ABC's Soup

Megan Kreplin
Coxsackie, NY

I enjoy making this warming soup on snowy winter afternoons. It can be served up in 20 minutes, just in time for everyone coming in from shoveling snow. Serve some hot Italian bread or Texas toast on the side to dip in the soup...there's nothing better!

1 T. olive oil
3/4 c. alphabet pasta, uncooked
1 clove garlic, minced
2 14-1/2 oz. cans chicken broth
8-oz. can tomato sauce

1/2 c. peas and/or diced carrots
Optional: grated Parmesan
   cheese, Italian-seasoned
   croutons

Heat oil in a saucepan over medium heat. Add uncooked pasta and garlic. Cook and stir for about 5 minutes, until pasta is golden. Stir in broth, tomato sauce and vegetables; bring to a boil. Cover and cook for about 10 minutes, until pasta is tender. Top each bowl with with Parmesan cheese and croutons, if desired. Makes 4 servings.

Simple Vegetable Soup

Marsha Good
Star City, IN

Growing up, my two sons preferred this to traditional vegetable soup...it was a much-liked way to get them to eat vegetables.

1 lb. ground beef
15-oz. can mixed vegetables
14-1/2 oz. can diced tomatoes

1 T. Worcestershire sauce
1 cube beef bouillon

Brown beef in a large saucepan over medium heat; drain. Add remaining ingredients; do not drain vegetables or tomatoes. Reduce heat to low. Cover and simmer for 10 to 15 minutes. Serves 3 to 4.

Good manners: The noise you don't make when you're eating soup.
−Bennett Cerf

Bean & Sausage Soup

Janice Marshall
Tucson, AZ

My dad just loves this soup! Your house will smell wonderful as it's cooking. Serve it with a big buttery piece of cornbread and you have a wonderful cool-weather meal.

1-1/2 lbs. mild or spicy Italian
  pork sausage links
2 T. olive oil
1/4 lb. prosciutto or deli ham,
  chopped
2 onions, chopped
3 carrots, peeled and chopped

3 stalks celery, chopped
1 t. ground thyme
3 15-oz. cans Great Northern
  beans, drained, rinsed
  and divided
4 c. chicken broth

In a large saucepan or soup pot over medium heat, cook sausage in olive oil until browned. Cut sausage into bite-size pieces; set aside in a bowl. Add prosciutto or ham, onions, carrots, celery and thyme to skillet; cook until soft. Mash one can of beans with a fork; add to pan along with remaining beans and broth. Return sausage to saucepan. Reduce heat to low; cover and simmer for about one hour, stirring occasionally. Serves 4 to 6.

Need to add a little zing to a pot of soup? Just add a splash of balsamic or herb-flavored vinegar...lemon juice works well also.

Carolyn's Toscana Soup

Carolyn Deckard
Bedford, IN

I love the Tuscan-style soup at everyone's favorite Italian restaurant, but could never find a recipe for it. This is the recipe my husband & I came up with a couple of years ago. We think it is delicious with garlic bread. Enjoy!

1/2 lb. spicy Italian pork
    sausage links
2-3/4 c. chicken broth
1/4 c. whipping cream
2 c. kale, chopped

2 russet potatoes, quartered
    and sliced
1/4 t. red pepper flakes
1/4 t. salt

Grill or sauté sausage until browned. Drain and cool; slice sausage at an angle, 1/2-inch thick. Combine broth and cream in a large saucepan over medium heat. Add sausage and remaining ingredients. Reduce heat to low. Cover and simmer for about one hour, stirring occasionally, until potatoes are tender. Serves 4.

Crisp, savory crackers are delightful alongside a steamy bowl
of soup. Spread saltines with softened butter and sprinkle with
Italian seasoning and garlic powder. Bake at 350 degrees
for just a few minutes, until golden.

Creamy Tomato Soup

Mel Chencharick
Julian, PA

A fantastic tomato soup! This recipe is best made with garden-fresh tomatoes in late summer, but canned tomatoes work well too.

4 c. tomatoes, diced
1 onion, chopped
3 whole cloves
3 sprigs fresh parsley
1 t. salt
1 t. pepper

1 t. brown sugar, packed
3 T. butter
3 T. all-purpose flour
1-1/2 c. chicken broth
1 c. half-and-half

In a soup pot over medium heat, combine tomatoes, onion, seasonings and brown sugar. Simmer for 10 minutes; remove from heat. With an immersion blender, process mixture to desired consistency. Melt butter in a saucepan over medium-low heat; add flour and stir until golden. Add broth to flour mixture; cook and stir until thickened. Add to tomato mixture; simmer for about 5 minutes. Cool slightly; stir in half-and-half. Gently heat through before serving. Makes 6 servings.

Creamy Potato Soup

Susan Lovelace
Gastonia, NC

Scrumptious topped with shredded cheese and bacon bits.

6 potatoes, peeled and diced
10-3/4 oz. can cream of chicken
   soup
12-oz. can evaporated milk

1 c. low-fat milk
1/4 to 1/2 c. butter, sliced
salt and pepper to taste

In a saucepan over medium-high heat, cover potatoes with water. Boil until falling apart when stirred, about 20 minutes. Drain, leaving just enough water to cover bottom of pan. In a bowl, mix chicken soup and evaporated milk; add to potatoes along with low-fat milk and butter. Bring to a boil; reduce heat to low. Simmer for 10 to 15 minutes. Season with salt and pepper. Add a little more milk if soup is too thick. Makes 6 servings.

Savory Simmering Soups

Spinach Tortellini Soup

Cyndy DeStefano
Mercer, PA

This quick & easy soup really hits the spot when it's cold outdoors.

2 48-oz. cans chicken broth
1 lb. ground beef
1 egg, beaten
1/2 c. seasoned dry bread
   crumbs
1 clove garlic, minced
16-oz. pkg. cheese tortellini,
   uncooked
10-oz. pkg. frozen chopped
   spinach, thawed

Pour broth into a large soup pot. Bring to a simmer over medium heat.
Meanwhile, in a bowl, mix beef, egg, bread crumbs and garlic. Form
into 3/4-inch balls. Drop meatballs into the simmering broth and cook
through, about 5 minutes. Add tortellini and cook about another
7 minutes, or as package directs. Stir in spinach and cook over low
heat for 3 to 4 minutes. Serves 8.

Rebecca's Fideo Soup

Rebecca Gonzalez
Moreno Valley, CA

I hadn't tried this recipe before my husband & I were married...
now I make it often during the winter and whenever the kids are
under the weather. It's very simple but very flavorful and filling.

3 roma tomatoes, quartered
1/2 onion
2 c. water
2 T. oil
8-oz. pkg. fideo vermicelli pasta,
   uncooked
Optional: 1 to 2 dried chile de
   arbol peppers
4 c. chicken broth
8-oz. can tomato sauce

Combine tomatoes, onion and water in a blender; process until smooth
and set aside. Heat oil in a large saucepan over medium-high heat;
add pasta and peppers, if using. Sauté until pasta turns a deep golden
color. Carefully add tomato mixture, broth and tomato sauce. Reduce
heat to low; cover and simmer until pasta is cooked through. Serves 6
to 8.

Chicken & Wild Rice Soup

Vickie

Wild rice and mushrooms give this hearty soup a rich, earthy taste.

2 T. butter
2 c. onion, diced
2 c. carrots, peeled and diced
1 c. celery, sliced
2 cloves garlic, diced
8 c. chicken broth
1 c. wild rice, uncooked
2 c. sliced mushrooms

2 bay leaves
1 t. dried thyme
1/2 c. white wine or chicken
    broth
2 c. cooked chicken breast, diced
salt and pepper to taste
Garnish: chopped fresh parsley

Melt butter in a large stockpot over medium heat. Add onion, carrots, celery and garlic; sauté until softened. Stir in broth, rice, mushrooms, bay leaves and thyme. Bring to a boil; reduce heat to low. Cover and simmer for about one hour, until rice is tender. Add wine or broth, chicken, salt and pepper; heat through. Garnish with parsley. Serves 6 to 8.

Variation:

Creamy Chicken & Wild Rice Soup: Stir in 1/2 cup half-and-half along with the wine or broth.

The earthy, nutty flavor of wild rice is delicious in soups, salads and sides. It's actually a grass seed, not a true rice, and takes a little longer to cook. When shopping, don't confuse it with already-seasoned mixes of wild rice and long-grain or brown rice.

Old-Fashioned Hamburger Soup

Pam Dodd
Greenwood, IN

*I've made this soup for 30 years. My family loves it year 'round,
no matter whether it's a cold winter day or the middle of summer.
Any leftovers will taste even better the next day!*

1 lb. lean ground beef	1/2 head cabbage, chopped
1 onion, diced	3 potatoes, peeled and diced
3 stalks celery, diced	16-oz. can kidney beans,
2 14-1/2 oz. cans diced	drained
tomatoes	4 cubes beef bouillon
3 c. water	1/4 t. garlic powder
11-1/2 oz. can cocktail	1/4 t. garlic salt
vegetable juice	salt and pepper to taste

Brown beef with onion and celery over medium heat in a large Dutch
oven or soup pot. Drain; add tomatoes with juice and remaining
ingredients. Bring to a boil; reduce heat to low. Cover and simmer for
1-1/2 hours, stirring occasionally, until vegetables are tender. Makes 8
to 10 servings.

Oops! If soup or stew starts to burn on the bottom, all is not lost. Spoon it
into another pan, being careful not to scrape up the scorched part on the
bottom. The burnt taste usually won't linger. To avoid burnt soup
the next time, cook over low heat and stir often.

Chicken Tortilla Soup

JoAnn

My friend Jeanne shared this recipe with me.

1 onion, chopped
2 T. garlic, minced
1 T. oil
2 t. ground cumin
1 T. chili powder
3 14-oz. cans chicken broth
4-oz. can green chiles, drained
14-1/2 oz. can diced tomatoes

15-oz. can black beans, drained
  and rinsed
10-oz. pkg. frozen corn
1 c. cooked chicken, diced
Garnish: sour cream, shredded
  Mexican-blend cheese,
  diced avocado

Sauté onion and garlic in oil in a stockpot over medium heat until
softened. Add spices; cook and stir for 2 minutes. Stir in broth, chiles
and tomatoes with juice. Reduce heat to low; cover and simmer for
20 to 30 minutes, stirring occasionally. Add beans, corn and chicken;
simmer until heated through. Garnish each soup bowl with Tortilla
Strips and desired toppings. Serves 8.

Tortilla Strips:

2 to 3 corn tortillas   coarse salt to taste

Slice tortillas into strips. Spray both sides with non-stick vegetable
spray. Place on an ungreased baking sheet. Bake at 350 degrees for
10 to 15 minutes, until crisp. Season with salt.

Cheesy quesadillas are quick and filling paired with soup. Sprinkle a flour
tortilla with shredded cheese, top with another tortilla and toast lightly
in a skillet until the cheese melts. Cut into wedges and serve with salsa.

Taco Beef Soup

Sharon Fehnel
Indianapolis, IN

This was my mother-in-law's recipe that I have tweaked over the years. She says now I make it better than she does! It's a family favorite for any get-together, but especially during football season.

1 lb. ground beef
1/4 c. onion
1-1/2 c. water
1-1/4 oz. pkg. taco
   seasoning mix
15-oz. can tomato sauce
14-1/2 oz. can stewed tomatoes

16-oz. can kidney beans
Optional: 1 avocado, halved,
   pitted and diced
Garnish: tortilla chips, sour
   cream, shredded Cheddar
   cheese, diced onion

In a large saucepan over medium heat, brown beef and onion; drain. Stir in water, taco seasoning, tomato sauce and undrained tomatoes and beans. Reduce heat to low. Cover and simmer at least 30 minutes, stirring occasionally. Add avocado, if using, just before serving. Serve in bowls, garnished with desired toppings. Serves 4 to 6.

Canned yellow or white hominy makes a tasty, filling addition to any southwestern-style soup. Simply drain, rinse and add to the soup pot.

Chicken Noodle Soup

Karen Grisham
Mukwonago, WI

A classic! I often make homemade bread to go along with this savory soup. It's a delicious way to use up leftover roast turkey too.

1 c. onion, chopped
1 c. celery, chopped
1/4 c. margarine
9 c. water
8 cubes chicken bouillon
4 c. cooked chicken, diced
1 c. carrots, peeled and diced

1/2 t. dry marjoram
1/4 t. pepper
1 bay leaf
2 c. medium egg noodles, uncooked
1 T. fresh parsley, chopped

In a soup pot over medium heat, cook onion and celery in margarine until tender, 4 to 5 minutes. Add water, bouillon, chicken, carrots and seasonings; bring to a boil. Reduce heat to low; cover and simmer about 30 minutes. Remove bay leaf; stir in noodles and parsley. Cook another 10 minutes, or until noodles are tender. Makes 6 servings.

It's best to remove bay leaves before serving your soup or stew.
Tuck them into a metal tea ball that can hang on the side of
the soup pot...easy to retrieve when done.

Hearty Chicken Stew

Annette Robinson
Fairmont Hot Springs, British Columbia

A much-requested dish from my family...nice to serve with homemade buns or biscuits.

4 slices bacon
2 t. olive oil
1 c. onion, chopped
6 cloves garlic, minced
1 c. celery, chopped
4 carrots, peeled and chopped
3 T. all-purpose flour
1-1/2 c. chicken broth

1/2 c. dry sherry or chicken broth
2 lbs. boneless, skinless chicken thighs, cubed
1 T. fresh thyme, snipped
1 c. frozen peas
1/4 c. light sour cream

In a large saucepan over medium heat, cook bacon until crisp. Drain; remove bacon to a paper towel-lined plate. Heat olive oil in the same skillet; add onion, garlic, celery and carrots. Cook, stirring occasionally, for about 5 minutes, until onion is soft. Sprinkle flour over vegetables; cook and stir for one minute. Stir in broth, wine or broth, chicken, bacon and thyme; bring to a boil. Reduce heat to medium-low. Simmer, uncovered, for about 25 minutes, until thickened and chicken is cooked. Stir in peas and sour cream; season with salt and pepper. Heat through. Makes 8 servings.

When frying bacon, prepare a few extra slices to tuck into the fridge. Combine with juicy slices of sun-ripened tomato, frilly lettuce and creamy mayonnaise for a fresh BLT sandwich... tomorrow's lunch is ready in a jiffy!

Quick Bean & Bacon Soup

Michelle Powell
Valley, AL

The kids love this soup, and I can serve it up in 30 minutes.
Use kitchen shears to make dicing the bacon a breeze.

1/2 lb. bacon, diced
1 onion, diced
1 stalk celery, diced
2 cloves garlic, minced

14-1/2 oz. can diced tomatoes,
   drained
2 15-oz. cans pork & beans
2 14-1/2 oz. cans beef broth

In a soup pot over medium heat, cook bacon until crisp. Drain most of the drippings; set aside bacon on a paper towel-lined plate. In remaining drippings, sauté onion, celery and garlic until tender. Stir in tomatoes, beans and broth; bring to a boil. Reduce heat to low; simmer, uncovered, for 15 minutes. Stir in bacon just before serving. Makes 6 servings.

Broccoli & Cheese Soup

Lauren Ayers
Atoka, TN

Delicious and so simple to make.

6 c. chicken broth
32-oz. pkg. frozen chopped
   broccoli
16-oz. pkg. pasteurized process
   cheese spread, cubed

1/2 c. cold water
1-1/2 t. cornstarch

Bring broth to a boil in a large saucepan over medium heat. Add broccoli. Return to a boil; cook until broccoli is tender, about 5 minutes. Add cheese and stir until melted. In a small jar, combine water and cornstarch; shake until cornstarch dissolves. Slowly add cornstarch mixture to soup. Cook and stir for several minutes, until thickened. Makes 6 to 8 servings.

Top bowls of hot soup with plain or cheesy popcorn
instead of croutons for a crunchy surprise.

Cabbage & Barley Soup

Carole Clark
Sterling Heights, MI

At a restaurant we had some soup made with cabbage and barley.
It was such a good soup...thick and very satisfying! I put together
this recipe that tastes very much like the one we enjoyed.

1/2 c. long-cooking pearled
   barley, uncooked
1/2 c. onion, diced
2 c. water
32-oz. container chicken broth

10-3/4 oz. can tomato soup
2 T. all-purpose flour
4 c. cabbage, coarsely shredded
3 T. sour cream

Combine barley, onion and water in a small saucepan over medium
heat. Cover and cook for about 45 minutes, until barley is soft; drain.
Meanwhile, in a soup pot, whisk together broth, tomato soup and flour.
For a thinner soup, add less flour. Add cabbage; simmer over medium-
low heat for about 20 minutes. When cabbage is almost soft, add
barley mixture. Place sour cream in a cup; whisk in several spoonfuls
of hot soup liquid until well combined. Add sour cream mixture to
soup. Cook and stir about 5 more minutes. Makes 4 to 6 servings.

Fantastic Tomato Florentine Soup

Amy Hunt
Traphill, NC

Quick and very tasty...dinner is ready in minutes!

2 to 3 c. small shell pasta,
   uncooked
4 10-3/4-oz. cans tomato soup
4 c. water
1/4 c. onion, diced

10-oz. pkg. frozen chopped
   spinach, thawed and well
   drained
salt and pepper to taste

Cook pasta as package directs; drain and return to saucepan. Add
remaining ingredients; heat through. Serves 8.

Watch for old-fashioned clear glass canisters at yard sales...
perfect countertop storage for pasta.

Meatless Minestrone

Erin Brock
Charleston, WV

Feel free to mix & match the veggies in this soup...it's a good way to use up odds & ends of veggies from the fridge. Diced zucchini and chopped spinach are great additions.

2 c. ditalini pasta, uncooked
1/2 c. onion, finely chopped
1 clove garlic, finely chopped
2 T. olive oil
5 c. vegetable broth
14-1/2 oz. can stewed tomatoes
1 c. cabbage, finely chopped
3/4 c. celery, finely chopped
15-1/2 oz. can cannellini beans, drained
1 t. Italian seasoning
1/4 t. pepper
1/4 c. shredded Parmesan cheese

Cook pasta as package directs; drain. Meanwhile, in a large saucepan over medium heat, cook onion and garlic in oil until tender. Add broth, tomatoes with juice, cabbage and celery. Bring to a boil; reduce heat to low. Simmer for about 20 minutes, stirring occasionally, until vegetables are tender. Stir in pasta, beans and seasonings; simmer for 5 minutes. Stir in Parmesan cheese. Makes 6 to 8 servings.

Tiny pasta shapes like ditalini, orzo, acini di pepe and stelline or stars are all quick-cooking and ideal for making soup. Choose your favorite... you can even substitute alphabets just for fun.

Weeknight Meatless Chili

Kimberly Ascroft
Rockledge, FL

*When it's chilly outside, I've worked all day and just don't
feel like cooking, this chili is a wonderful solution!*

15-1/2 oz. can diced tomatoes
15-1/2 oz. can kidney beans,
   drained
15-1/2 oz. can Great Northern
   beans, drained
15-oz. can garbanzo beans,
   drained
28-oz. can tomato sauce

1-3/4 c. water
3 T. chili powder
1 T. onion powder
1-1/2 t. paprika
salt and pepper to taste
Garnish: shredded Cheddar
   cheese, sour cream

In a Dutch oven over medium-high heat, combine undrained tomatoes
and remaining ingredients except garnish. Bring to a boil; reduce heat
to low. Cover and simmer for 45 minutes, stirring occasionally, until
beans are soft. Top each soup bowl with cheese and sour cream.
Makes 6 to 8 servings.

Serve chili Cincinnati-style! For 2-way chili, ladle chili over a bowl of
spaghetti. For 3-way, top chili and spaghetti with shredded Cheddar
cheese. For 4-way, spoon diced onions on top of the cheese...
add chili beans to the stack for 5-way.

Hearty Fisherman's Stew

Eleanor Dionne
Beverly, MA

*My mother used to make this recipe often
for our meatless Friday meals.*

1-1/2 c. celery, chopped
1/2 c. onion, chopped
1 clove garlic, minced
1/4 c. butter
14-oz. can whole tomatoes
8-oz. can tomato sauce
1/2 t. paprika
1/2 t. chili powder

2 t. salt
1/4 t. pepper
2 c. boiling water
8-oz. pkg. spaghetti, uncooked
2 lbs. haddock or cod, cut into
   1-inch cubes
Garnish: grated Parmesan
   cheese

In a large deep saucepan over medium heat, sauté celery, onion and
garlic in butter until tender. Add tomatoes with juice, tomato sauce and
seasonings; bring to a simmer. Reduce heat to low; cover and cook for
20 minutes, stirring occasionally. Increase heat to medium. Add boiling
water and uncooked spaghetti; stir. Cook for about 10 minutes, stirring
often, until spaghetti is almost tender. Add fish. Cover and cook over
low heat for about 10 minutes, until fish flakes easily with a fork.
Serve sprinkled with Parmesan cheese. Makes 6 to 8 servings.

Eat-it-all bread bowls make hearty soup extra special. Cut the tops off
round loaves of bread and hollow out, then rub with olive oil and garlic.
Pop bread bowls in the oven at 400 degrees for 10 minutes, or until
crusty and golden. Ladle in soup and enjoy!

VEGETABLE
Side Dishes

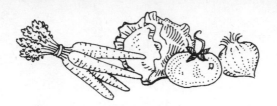

Grandma's Baked Mac & Cheese

Krista Marshall
Fort Wayne, IN

My grandma has been making this for years, and now it's my go-to dish for busy weeknights. It's a real crowd-pleaser! You don't even have to pre-cook the macaroni. Cut leftovers into individual portions, wrap and freeze for quick lunches.

2 c. elbow macaroni, uncooked
4 c. milk
salt and pepper to taste

2-1/2 c. shredded sharp Cheddar cheese, divided

In a greased 13"x9" baking pan, mix uncooked macaroni, milk, salt, pepper and 1/2 cup cheese. Sprinkle remaining cheese over top. Bake, uncovered, at 375 degrees for 45 minutes to one hour, until bubbly, golden and macaroni is tender. Serves 8.

Love a crunchy golden crumb topping on your macaroni & cheese?
Toss some soft fresh bread crumbs with a little melted butter and
sprinkle them on the unbaked casserole before baking.

Tomatoes Creole

Donna Clement
Daphne, AL

*Living in New Orleans for years and then moving to southern
Alabama gave me a taste of some of the best dishes
in America. Southerners can really cook!*

1/2 c. fresh parsley, chopped
2 cloves garlic, chopped
6 tomatoes, sliced 1/4-inch thick
salt and pepper to taste

1/4 c. butter, sliced
1-1/4 c. seasoned dry bread
   crumbs
grated Parmesan cheese to taste

Mix together parsley and garlic in a small bowl; set aside. Arrange
tomato slices in a buttered 13"x9" baking pan. Season tomatoes with
salt and pepper; dot with butter. Sprinkle with parsley mixture, bread
crumbs and Parmesan cheese. Bake, uncovered, at 350 degrees for
30 minutes, or until bubbly and golden. Makes 4 to 6 servings.

Serve up a Southern-style vegetable plate for dinner. With two or three
scrumptious veggie dishes and a basket of buttery cornbread,
no one will even miss the meat.

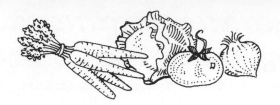

Sue's Best Green Beans

Sue Neely
Greenville, IL

Here is an old family recipe for the most delicious green beans you'll taste. Have a spatula ready to protect your share...they are the best!

2 T. bacon drippings, or
    1 T. butter plus 1 T. olive oil
1 c. onion, chopped
2 cloves garlic, minced
1 lb. fresh green beans, trimmed

1 c. chicken broth
1/2 c. red pepper, chopped
1/4 to 1/2 t. salt
pepper to taste

Melt drippings or butter and oil in a skillet over medium-low heat. Add onion and garlic; cook and stir for one minute. Add beans; cook for one minute, or until beans turn bright green. Add broth, red pepper, salt and pepper. Reduce heat to low. Cover, leaving lid tilted slightly to allow steam to escape. Cook for 20 to 30 minutes, until liquid evaporates, beans are crisp-tender and onion and pepper are caramelized. A little more broth may be added during cooking, if needed. Serves 4.

Blanching makes fresh veggies like green beans crisp and bright... super for salads and dips. Bring a large pot of salted water to a rolling boil, add trimmed veggies and boil for 3 to 4 minutes, just until they begin to soften. Immediately remove veggies to a bowl of ice water. Cool, drain and pat dry.

Golden Parmesan Potatoes

Becky Holsinger
Belpre, OH

*I'm always looking for new ways to fix potatoes. I found
this recipe and really like it...it's easy and delicious!*

2 lbs. new potatoes, quartered
1/4 c. olive oil
1-1/2 t. Italian seasoning

2 cloves garlic, minced
1/3 c. grated Parmesan cheese

In a large bowl, toss potatoes with oil, seasoning and garlic. Add
cheese; mix lightly. Spread mixture in a lightly greased 15"x10"
jelly-roll pan. Bake, uncovered, at 400 degrees for 45 minutes,
or until potatoes are tender. Makes 6 servings.

If you use lots of Italian seasoning, mix up your own to store in a
shaker jar...you may already have the ingredients in your spice rack.
A good basic blend is 2 tablespoons each of dried oregano, basil,
thyme, marjoram and rosemary. Add or subtract to suit your taste.

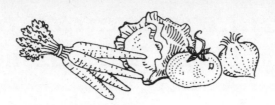

Grandpa's Squash Skillet

Michelle Blair-Weeks
Santa Rosa, CA

My grandfather had a garden every year with an abundance of zucchini and the best beefsteak tomatoes. He used to make this side dish to use his fresh vegetables. It's a recipe that he made up on his own, as far as I know.

1/2 red onion, thinly sliced
1 clove garlic, minced
2 t. butter
2 yellow squash, thinly sliced
2 crookneck squash, thinly
   sliced
3 zucchini, thinly sliced

1/2 lb. sliced mushrooms
salt and pepper to taste
2 to 3 ripe tomatoes, thickly
   sliced
4 to 5 slices sharp Cheddar
   cheese

In a large skillet over medium-low heat, sauté onion and garlic in butter for 4 to 5 minutes. Layer squash and mushrooms in skillet; season with salt and pepper. Add tomatoes in a single layer. Cover and simmer to desired doneness, 10 to 15 minutes. Arrange cheese slices over tomatoes. Simmer until cheese melts and serve immediately. Serves 4 to 6.

Jot down favorite recipes, ones that have been handed down, and make copies to share when family & friends are together. It's a terrific way to preserve those that are time-tested and bring back the sweetest memories.

Italian Zucchini

Stephanie Gegg
Sainte Genevieve, MO

I love summer gardening and all my fresh produce! This makes a great side dish at any barbecue. I've even enjoyed it as my main dish...it's a satisfying meatless meal.

1-1/2 c. zucchini, cubed
15-1/2 oz. can petite diced
   tomatoes
1 c. sweet onion, chopped
1 c. sliced mushrooms

1/2 t. garlic, minced
1/2 t. red pepper flakes
1/8 t. dried oregano
1/2 t. salt
1/8 t. pepper

Combine zucchini, undrained tomatoes and remaining ingredients in a medium saucepan. Cook over medium heat for 20 to 25 minutes, until vegetables are tender. Makes 4 servings.

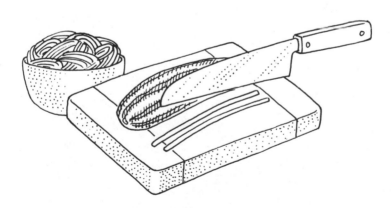

For a delicious, healthy change from regular pasta, make "noodles" from zucchini or summer squash. Cut the squash into long, thin strips, steam lightly or sauté in a little olive oil and toss with your favorite pasta sauce.

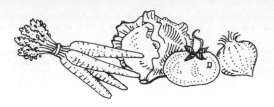

French Rice

Michelle Lockett
Lebam, WA

An easy side dish to pop in the oven...who needs a boxed mix?

1 c. long-cooking rice, uncooked
4-oz. can sliced mushrooms, drained
1/2 c. onion, chopped
10-1/2 oz. can French onion soup

1 c. beef consommé
1/2 c. butter, melted
1/3 c. water
1 T. fresh parsley, chopped
1 clove garlic, minced

Combine all ingredients in a lightly greased 2-quart casserole dish. Stir gently. Cover and bake at 350 degrees for 35 minutes, or until liquid is absorbed and rice is tender. Makes 4 to 5 servings.

Here's a little trick to clean baked-on food from a casserole dish.
Place a dryer sheet inside and fill with water. Let the dish sit overnight,
then sponge clean. You'll find the fabric softeners will really
soften the baked-on food.

Savory Braised Kale

JoAnn

*An easy and flavorful way to prepare green leafy vegetables...
try it with Swiss chard too!*

2 to 3 slices bacon
1-1/4 c. onion, thinly sliced
1 lb. fresh kale, chopped
1/3 c. apple cider or apple juice
1 T. cider vinegar

1-1/2 c. tart apple, peeled,
  cored and diced
1/2 t. salt
1/4 t. pepper

In a large skillet over medium heat, cook bacon until crisp, about
5 minutes. Remove bacon to a paper towel-lined plate, reserving
drippings in skillet. Crumble bacon and set aside. Increase heat to
medium-high. Add onion to skillet; cook until tender, about 5 minutes.
Add kale; cook until wilted, about 5 minutes, stirring often. Sprinkle
cider and vinegar over kale. Reduce heat to low; cover and cook for
10 minutes, stirring occasionally. Add apple; cook until apple is tender.
Season with salt and pepper. At serving time, sprinkle with crumbled
bacon. Serves 6.

Fresh greens are tasty and packed with nutrients...they're easy to
mix & match in recipes too. Try spinach, kale, Swiss chard, turnip greens,
broccoli rabe or peppery mustard greens, added to stir-fries or just
simmered in broth with a little sautéed onion.

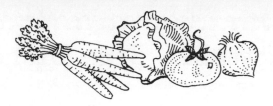

Hawaiian Baked Beans

Debra Elliott
Birmingham, AL

My children love pineapple and baked beans, so I thought,
"Why not combine the two into a yummy side dish?" I created
this recipe 25 years ago, and it's still a family favorite.

1-3/4 c. pineapple juice
1 c. catsup
1/2 c. mustard
1-1/2 c. dark brown sugar,
    packed

15-oz. can pineapple chunks,
    drained
4 15-1/2 oz. cans navy beans &
    bacon, drained and rinsed

In a bowl, whisk together pineapple juice, catsup and mustard. Add
brown sugar and mix well; stir in pineapple chunks. Add beans; mix
well. Spoon into a greased 13"x9" baking pan. Bake, uncovered, at
350 degrees for 90 minutes, or until hot and bubbly. Serves 8 to 12.

Yummiest Applesauce

Sharman Hess
Asheville, NC

This applesauce has become an annual side on Thanksgiving.
The recipe is easily doubled if one needs additional servings.

4 Granny Smith apples, peeled,
    cored and diced
1 c. water
1/2 c. brown sugar, packed
1 T. butter

1/4 t. cinnamon
1/8 t. nutmeg
3/4 c. chopped walnuts
1/2 c. golden raisins

Place apples and water in a saucepan over medium heat; bring to a
boil. Reduce heat to low. Simmer, stirring occasionally, for 10 to
15 minutes, until apples are tender. Stir in remaining ingredients;
heat through until raisins are plump. Makes 4 servings.

Laughter is brightest where food is best.
— Irish Proverb

Orange-Maple Carrots

Justin Prather
Marietta, GA

My family always finds this dish to exhibit the three F's...fast, flavorful and fabulous! The dish may be stored in the fridge and reheated later. You can also use baby carrots, just steam them a little longer.

12 carrots, peeled and thinly
    sliced
1/2 c. water
1/3 c. orange juice
zest of one orange

3 T. maple syrup
2 T. dark brown sugar, packed
2 T. butter
1/4 t. nutmeg

Place carrots in a large deep saucepan; add water. Bring to a boil over medium heat. Reduce heat; cover and cook until carrots are crisp-tender, about 5 minutes. Drain; cover and set aside. In a separate saucepan, combine remaining ingredients. Stir; heat through just until boiling. Remove from heat; pour mixture over carrots and mix together very well. Makes 4 to 5 servings.

A dollop of lemon butter adds flavor to plain steamed vegetables.
Simply blend 2 tablespoons softened butter with the zest of one lemon.

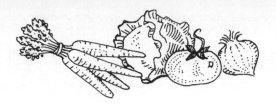

Swiss Scalloped Potatoes

Shirley Howie
Foxboro, MA

These potatoes are delicious and so quick & easy to make! A go-to recipe that is always welcome at potlucks and family get-togethers.

6 c. new potatoes, thinly sliced and divided
1/2 c. onion, finely chopped and divided
2 c. shredded Swiss cheese, divided

salt and pepper to taste
1 T. beef bouillon granules
1 c. boiling water

In a greased shallow 1-1/2 quart casserole dish, layer half the potato slices, half the onion and half the cheese. Sprinkle lightly with salt and pepper; repeat layers. Stir bouillon into boiling water; pour over potatoes and cheese. Bake, uncovered, at 400 degrees for 45 to 50 minutes, until potatoes are tender and crust is golden. Let stand 5 minutes before serving. Serves 6.

For a crispy, crunchy casserole topping, leave the casserole dish uncovered while it's baking. Cover it if you prefer a softer consistency.

Vegetable Side Dishes

Cashew-Topped Broccoli

Irene Robinson
Cincinnati, OH

Our family loves this veggie dish with baked ham or pork chops.

2 10-oz. pkgs. frozen broccoli
   spears, thawed
10-3/4 oz. can cream of
   celery soup

1 c. salted cashews
1 t. dried, minced onion
1/2 c. shredded Monterey
   jack cheese

Arrange broccoli spears in a greased 13"x9" baking pan. Combine remaining ingredients in a bowl; spoon over broccoli. Bake, uncovered, at 350 degrees for 30 minutes, or until hot and bubbly. Serves 6.

Broccoli-Rice Bake

Nina Ash
Hant's Harbour, Newfoundland

I like to add diced red or yellow peppers for a pop of color.

2 c. broccoli flowerets, chopped
1 c. onion, chopped
2 T. butter
10-3/4 oz. can cream of
   mushroom soup

1/2 c. plus 2 T. milk
1 c. long-cooking rice, uncooked
1/2 c. shredded Cheddar cheese

Cover broccoli with water in a saucepan. Cook over medium heat until tender; drain. Meanwhile, in a small skillet over medium heat, cook onion in butter until tender. In a bowl, blend together soup and milk. Combine broccoli, onion mixture, soup mixture and uncooked rice in a greased 2-quart casserole dish. Top with cheese. Bake, uncovered, at 350 degrees for 30 minutes, or until hot and bubbly. Serves 6.

After groceries are unpacked, take just a little time to chop fruits and vegetables and place them in plastic zipping bags. Weeknight dinners will be so much easier.

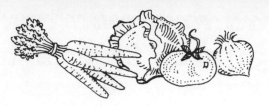

Amy's 2-Squash Delight

Amy Jones
Graham, NC

After we started harvesting our first garden, I came up with this recipe...it's so delicious, it's a new summer tradition!

1 yellow squash, diced
1 zucchini, diced
14-1/2 oz. can fire-roasted diced
   tomatoes

2 T. extra-virgin olive oil
1 t. Italian seasoning
Garnish: grated Parmesan
   cheese

In a skillet, combine squash, zucchini, undrained tomatoes, oil and seasoning. Simmer over medium heat until squash is tender. Top with Parmesan cheese before serving. Makes 4 servings.

Make a frosty pitcher of strawberry lemonade. Combine a 12-ounce can of frozen lemonade concentrate, a 10-ounce package of frozen strawberries and 4-1/2 cups of cold water. Let stand until berries thaw, then stir well. Wonderful!

Nani's Mac & Cheese

Starla Smith
Manhattan Beach, CA

I was never a fan of homemade mac & cheese until my mother-in-law served this one night. When I tried it, I was hooked! Then I tweaked the recipe to make a savory version...now it's my go-to dish to bring to all the holiday dinners! Either way, it's delicious and satisfying.

16-oz. pkg. elbow or small shell macaroni, uncooked
12-oz. can evaporated milk
1 c. water
2 T. cornstarch
2 T. butter
1/2 t. salt
1/4 t. pepper
16-oz. pkg. shredded sharp Cheddar cheese

Cook macaroni according to package instructions; drain. Place macaroni in a 13"x9" baking pan sprayed with non-stick vegetable spray and set aside. Meanwhile, in a large saucepan, combine remaining ingredients except cheese. Bring to a boil over medium heat. Boil for one minute; remove from heat. Add cheese; stir until completely melted. Spoon cheese mixture over macaroni; mix well. Bake, uncovered, at 375 degrees for 20 minutes, or until bubbly and golden. Serves 10 to 15.

Variation:

Starla's Savory Mac & Cheese: Cook macaroni; place in baking pan as directed above. In a large saucepan, sauté one diced sweet onion in one tablespoon olive oil until tender. Add one to 2 cups diced cooked ham; cook for one to 2 minutes. Add remaining ingredients above, except cheese; bring to a boil. Finish recipe as directed, replacing sharp Cheddar cheese with 1-1/2 cups each shredded Cheddar and Pepper Jack cheese.

Brighten a dinner plate with edible fruit and veggie garnishes...
try carrot curls, radish roses, pineapple spears or kiwi slices.

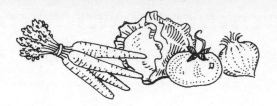

Honey-Glazed Vegetables

Lisa Ann Panzino-DiNunzio
Vineland, NJ

The only comment I hear when serving this delicious side dish is, "More, please!" You can use a variety of your own favorite vegetables as you wish.

2 c. fresh green beans
2 c. fresh broccoli flowerets
1 bunch fresh asparagus, trimmed
1 Spanish onion, cut into wedges
2 c. whole mushrooms, halved
4 cloves garlic, chopped
1/4 c. extra-virgin olive oil
salt and pepper to taste
1/4 c. balsamic vinegar
3 to 4 T. honey

Place vegetables and garlic in a large bowl; toss with olive oil. Spread mixture on a lightly greased 15"x10" jelly-roll pan; sprinkle with salt and pepper. Bake, uncovered, at 400 degrees for about 35 minutes, stirring occasionally, until lightly golden and fork-tender. Meanwhile, heat vinegar in a small saucepan over low heat for about 5 minutes, until reduced slightly. Remove from heat; stir in honey. Remove vegetables from oven and drizzle with vinegar mixture. Stir again; bake an additional 8 to 10 minutes. Makes 6 to 8 servings.

Keep baking soda on hand for cleaning soil, wax and residue from fresh fruit and vegetables. Sprinkle a little baking soda on a sponge, scrub gently and rinse with cool water...no fancy produce washes needed.

Oven Potatoes

Wendy White
Lower Hainesville, New Brunswick

These seasoned potatoes are so simple to fix and almost mess-free...mix in a plastic bag, then just toss away the bag.

6 russet potatoes, peeled and
    cut into wedges or cubes
2 T. olive oil
1 t. dried, minced onion

1 t. garlic powder
1 t. dried oregano
1 t. paprika
1/2 t. salt

Place potatoes in a large plastic zipping bag or a bowl. Sprinkle with remaining ingredients; shake or stir to mix. Spread potatoes onto an aluminum foil-lined 15"x10" jelly-roll pan. Bake, uncovered, at 400 degrees for 30 to 40 minutes, stirring occasionally, until crisp and golden. Serves 6.

Potatoes come in three basic types. Starchy russet potatoes bake up fluffy and are great for frying too. Round waxy potatoes are excellent in soups, casseroles and potato salads. All-purpose potatoes are in between and work well in most recipes. Do some delicious experimenting to find your favorites!

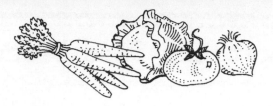

Zesty Italian Rice

Jill Valentine
Jackson, TN

We enjoy this versatile dish alongside grilled chicken or sausage.

1/4 c. onion, diced
1/2 c. green pepper, chopped
1 t. garlic, minced
2 t. olive oil
1 c. long-cooking rice, uncooked
14-1/2 oz. can vegetable broth

1/2 c. roasted red pepper,
    drained and diced
1/2 c. petite diced tomatoes,
    drained
1/2 t. dried oregano
1/2 t. dried basil

In a large saucepan over medium heat, sauté onion, green pepper and garlic in olive oil for 3 minutes. Add rice; cook and stir until lightly golden, about 5 minutes. Stir in remaining ingredients; bring to a boil. Reduce heat; cover and simmer for 20 minutes, or until rice is tender. Remove from heat. Let stand, covered, for 5 minutes. Fluff with a fork before serving. Makes 4 servings.

Variation:

Spicy Southwestern Rice: Prepare as directed above, using diced tomatoes with chiles or jalapeños instead of plain tomatoes. Season with chili powder and cumin instead of oregano and basil. If desired, top with 3/4 cup shredded Monterey Jack cheese after removing from heat.

Get the most flavor from
dried herbs...simply rub them
together between your
fingers to release the oils.

Marsha's Zucchini-Tomato Bake

Marsha Kent
Chapin, SC

*This side dish is easy to prepare, yet always gets
great compliments at gatherings.*

4 zucchini, sliced 1/2-inch thick
4 tomatoes, cubed
1 T. olive oil
1/4 c. shredded Parmesan
   cheese

Herbes de Provence or dried
   thyme to taste

Arrange zucchini slices in a lightly greased 13"x9" baking pan; top
with tomatoes. Drizzle tomatoes with olive oil; sprinkle with Parmesan
cheese and herbs. Bake, uncovered, at 350 degrees for 35 to
45 minutes. Serves 4 to 6.

Keep cutting boards smelling fresh simply by rubbing them
thoroughly with lemon wedges...it works for hands too!

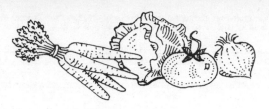

Zesty Smashed Cauliflower

Sandy Geiger
Columbia City, IN

A tasty alternative to mashed potatoes!

1 head cauliflower, cut into
   flowerets
3 to 4 T. water
3/4 c. ranch-flavored
   sour cream dip

1/4 c. grated Parmesan cheese
1/2 t. garlic, minced
salt and pepper to taste
2 T. butter, softened

Place cauliflower in a microwave-safe dish; add water. Cover and microwave on high setting until soft, about 8 to 10 minutes. Drain well; cool slightly. Transfer cauliflower to a blender or food processor; add dip, cheese, garlic, salt and pepper. Process until nearly smooth; stir in butter. Makes 4 servings.

Going to the farmers' market? Bring along an ice chest and
several ice packs if you won't be returning home right away.
Perishable produce will stay fresh and crisp.

Oven-Roasted Broccoli & Pine Nuts

Jessica Kraus
Delaware, OH

Roasted broccoli with a light lemon flavor. Don't care for pine nuts? Use walnuts instead...or just omit the nuts!

1 bunch broccoli, cut into
   flowerets
juice of 1 lemon
2 T. olive oil

salt and pepper to taste
1/4 c. grated Parmesan cheese
1/4 c. pine nuts, toasted

In a large bowl, combine broccoli, lemon juice and olive oil. Season with salt and pepper; toss to mix. Spread mixture on a lightly greased 15"x10" jelly-roll pan. Bake, uncovered, at 425 degrees for 25 minutes, or until broccoli is tender. Remove from oven; toss with Parmesan cheese and pine nuts. Serves 4.

Toasty Garlic Cauliflower

Cheri Maxwell
Gulf Breeze, FL

My boys refused to eat cooked cauliflower. Then I served it to them prepared this way...they loved it!

1 head cauliflower, cut into
   flowerets
3 T. olive oil
2 T. garlic, minced

salt and pepper to taste
1/3 c. grated Parmesan cheese
1 T. fresh parsley, chopped

Combine cauliflower, olive oil and garlic in a plastic zipping bag; shake to coat. Spread mixture on a lightly greased 15"x10" jelly-roll pan; season with salt and pepper. Bake at 450 degrees for 25 minutes, stirring after 15 minutes. Remove from oven; top with cheese and parsley. Broil for 3 to 5 minutes, until golden. Serves 6.

Use a crinkle cutter to jazz up zucchini, carrots and other sliced veggies.

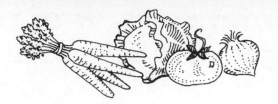

Cheesy Cottage Potatoes

Marsha Baker
Pioneer, OH

This is a casserole my mom always made when I was growing up.
Now my family requests it often for family meals...my daughters-in-
law especially like it. It's delicious and comforting.

10 russet potatoes
1 onion, chopped
8-oz. pkg. pasteurized process
   cheese, cubed
1 slice fresh bread, torn into
   bite-size pieces

1/2 t. salt
Optional: 2-oz. jar pimentos,
   drained
1/2 c. butter, melted and divided
1/4 c. milk
2 c. corn flake cereal, crushed

In a stockpot, cover unpeeled potatoes with water. Bring to a boil over
high heat. Cook until tender, 15 to 20 minutes. Drain and cool; peel
potatoes and cut into cubes. In a large bowl, combine potatoes, onion,
cheese, bread, salt and pimentos, if using. Drizzle with 6 tablespoons
butter. Spoon mixture into a lightly greased 2-1/2 quart casserole dish.
Drizzle milk over top. In a small bowl, combine crushed cereal with
remaining butter; spread evenly over potato mixture. Bake, uncovered,
at 350 degrees for 35 to 45 minutes, until bubbly and topping is
golden. If making ahead of time, do not add milk and topping until
just before baking. Makes 8 servings.

Moderation. Small helpings. Sample a little bit of everything.
These are the secrets of happiness and good health.
– Julia Child

Country Skillet Cabbage

Suzanne Varnes
Palatka, FL

This is my version of a family recipe that was given to my mom by her cousin. For a vegetarian version, omit the bacon and sauté vegetables in 2 to 3 tablespoons olive oil.

3 to 5 slices bacon, diced
1 onion, chopped
2 carrots, peeled and sliced
1 head cabbage, coarsely
   chopped

1 green pepper, diced
2 stalks celery, chopped
2 c. tomatoes, diced
1/4 c. lemon juice, or to taste
salt, pepper and sugar to taste

In a large skillet over medium-high heat, cook bacon until it just starts to brown. Do not drain. Add onion, carrots and cabbage to bacon and drippings in skillet. Sauté over medium-high heat until onion and carrot begin to soften. Stir in remaining ingredients; bring to a boil. Reduce heat to medium-low. Cover and simmer, stirring occasionally, until vegetables are tender-crisp, about 15 minutes. Serves 6 to 8.

For twice the juice, microwave lemons for 30 seconds
before juicing...it works with limes too!

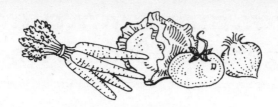

Tried & True Orzo-Rice Pilaf

Judy Henfey
Cibolo, TX

A very simple side to make when you are grilling chicken, beef or vegetables. It was one of the first dishes I served at a dinner party, and I still enjoy it. Easy peasy!

1/2 c. butter
1 c. orzo pasta, uncooked
4 c. water

1 c. long-cooking rice, uncooked
3 cubes chicken bouillon
salt and pepper to taste

Melt butter in a saucepan over medium heat; add pasta. Cook, stirring often, until golden, about 10 minutes. Stir in water, rice and bouillon cubes. Bring to a boil; reduce heat to low. Cover and simmer for 30 minutes, or until liquid is absorbed and pasta and rice are tender. Season with salt and pepper. Serves 4 to 6.

Bouillon cubes are an easy substitute for canned chicken and beef broth. To make one cup of broth, dissolve a bouillon cube in one cup of boiling water. Use 1-3/4 cups prepared bouillon to replace a 14-ounce can of broth.

Lima Beans & Bacon

Caroline Pacheco
Plant City, FL

This is the only way my kids will eat lima beans!

4 slices bacon
10-oz. pkg. frozen baby lima
    beans
2 stalks celery, thinly sliced

1/2 onion, chopped
1/4 t. salt
1/8 t. pepper
1/3 c. chicken broth

In a skillet, cook bacon over medium heat until crisp. Drain bacon on paper towels; reserve one tablespoon drippings in skillet. Add frozen beans, celery, onion, salt and pepper to bacon drippings. Cook, stirring often, until vegetables are tender, about 5 minutes. Increase heat to high; stir in broth and bring to a boil. Reduce heat to low; simmer for 5 minutes. Spoon mixture into a serving bowl; top with crumbled bacon. Serves 4.

Farmhouse Creamed Peas

Renae Scheiderer
Beallsville, OH

This is a favorite side dish in our house...it goes together so quickly!

10-oz. pkg. frozen peas
1 T. butter
1 T. all-purpose flour
1/4 t. salt

1/8 t. pepper
1/2 c. milk
1 t. sugar

Cook peas according to package directions. Meanwhile, in a small saucepan over low heat, melt butter. Stir in flour, salt and pepper until blended; gradually add milk and sugar. Bring to a boil; cook and stir for one to 2 minutes, until thickened. Drain peas; add to sauce and heat through. Serves 3 to 4.

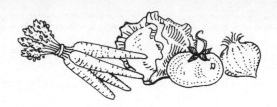

Surprise Scalloped Corn

Jana Temple
Colorado Springs, CO

This is my mother's recipe that has been handed down to me and now to my grown daughters. It is very special to us. She passed away some time ago, and I am happy to share it in her honor.

14-3/4 oz. can cream-style corn
15-oz. can corn, drained
1/4 c. butter, melted and slightly
    cooled
8-1/2 oz. pkg. corn muffin mix

2 eggs, beaten
1/4 c. sugar
8-oz. container sour cream
1 c. shredded Cheddar cheese

In a large bowl, mix together all ingredients. Spoon into a greased 3-quart casserole dish. Batter will rise slightly during baking, so make sure there is 1/2 to one-inch space in dish above batter. Bake, uncovered, at 350 degrees for 50 to 60 minutes, until golden. Serves 4 to 6.

Keep a couple of favorite side dishes tucked away in the freezer.
Pair with hot sandwiches or a deli roast chicken to put
a hearty homestyle meal on the table in a hurry.

Country Green Beans

Lori Palmer
East Alton, IL

For family get-togethers, I like to make a double or triple batch of this recipe. Everyone always loves the fresh-from-the-farm taste! Crisply cooked crumbled bacon may be used instead of ham.

1/4 c. butter, sliced
1/4 c. chicken broth
1 lb. fresh green beans, trimmed
1/4 c. onion, chopped

1/4 c. cooked ham, chopped
1 clove garlic, minced
1/2 t. salt
1/4 t. pepper

In a saucepan over medium-low heat, combine all ingredients. Cover and simmer for 15 to 20 minutes, until beans are tender. Serves 4 to 6.

How to know whether to start fresh vegetables cooking in hot or cold water? Old kitchen wisdom says to start vegetables that grow above the ground in boiling water...below the ground, in cold water.

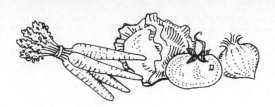

Mom's Dutch Noodles

Janet Powell McKee
Manteca, CA

This was one of my mom's favorite dishes when we were growing up.
It is still is a favorite of our children and grandchildren.

16-oz. pkg. homestyle egg
    noodles, uncooked
4 c. chicken broth
1 T. salt

1/4 lb. bacon, diced
1/2 onion, chopped
Optional: 1 c. dry bread crumbs

Cook noodles according to package directions, adding broth and salt
to cooking water; drain. Meanwhile, add bacon to a large skillet over
medium heat; cook until bacon is golden but not crisp and onion is
translucent. Add noodles to bacon mixture. Cook for 5 to 7 minutes,
tossing occasionally. Top with crumbs, if desired. Serves 4 to 6.

Parmesan Noodles

Stephanie Hilling
Morgantown, WV

My two young boys both love noodles of every variety. I was getting
tired of making the same old noodles with broth and wanted
something different. Voilà, a speedy side the whole family enjoys!
My husband even requests these as the main dinner entree.

8-oz. pkg. wide egg noodles,
    uncooked
3 T. butter, sliced

1/4 c. grated Parmesan cheese
1 t. dried parsley
salt and pepper to taste

Cook noodles according to package directions; drain and return to pan.
Add remaining ingredients to noodles. Stir to mix well, just until butter
and cheese melt, returning to very low heat if needed. Additional
butter and cheese may be added, if desired. Serves 4.

Comfort-Food
MAIN DISHES

Mom's Skillet Swiss Steak

Anett Yeager
La Center, WA

My mom used to make this weekly...now my family asks for it often.

1 lb. beef sirloin tip steak or
   bottom round steak
3 T. all-purpose flour
3 T. butter
2 8-oz. cans tomato sauce
1 T. Worcestershire sauce

1 T. soy sauce
1 T. lemon juice
1 onion, sliced
1 green pepper, sliced
cooked rice or noodles

Thinly slice beef across the grain into strips. Lightly coat beef with flour. Melt butter in a large skillet over medium heat; brown beef, one-half at a time. Return all beef to skillet. Add sauces and lemon juice; mix well. Add onion and green pepper. Cover and simmer for 45 minutes, or until beef is tender, stirring occasionally. Serve over rice or noodles. Serves 4.

Food for friends doesn't have to be fancy...your guests will be thrilled with old-fashioned comfort foods. Let everyone help themselves from big platters set right on the table. They'll love it!

Sour Cream Noodle Bake

Sandy Coffey
Cincinnati, OH

*Delicious and quick to fix when time is limited...a real
comfort food for frosty winter evenings.*

8-oz. pkg. wide egg noodles,
  uncooked
1 lb. ground beef
8-oz. can tomato sauce
1/4 t. garlic powder
1 t. salt
1/8 t. pepper
1 c. cottage cheese
1 c. sour cream
1 T. butter, melted
6 green onions, chopped
3/4 c. shredded Cheddar cheese

Cook noodles according to package directions; drain. Meanwhile, in a
skillet over medium heat, brown beef; drain. Stir tomato sauce, garlic
powder, salt and pepper into beef; simmer for 5 minutes. Add cottage
cheese, sour cream, butter and onions to noodles; mix gently. In a
greased 2-quart casserole dish, alternate layers of noodle mixture
and beef mixture; top with shredded cheese. Bake, uncovered,
at 350 degrees for 20 minutes, or until cheese is melted and golden.
Makes 6 to 8 servings.

When making a favorite casserole, why not make a double batch?
After baking, let the extra casserole cool, wrap and tuck it in the freezer...
ready to share with a new mother, carry to a potluck or
reheat on a busy night at home.

Butter-Roasted Chicken

Stephanie Monroe
Franklin, TN

You'll love this savory golden chicken...it takes very little effort to prepare.

10 bone-in chicken thighs	2 t. salt
1 c. water	1 t. pepper
1/2 c. lemon juice	1 t. dried rosemary
2 T. butter, sliced	1 t. chicken bouillon granules
2 T. paprika	1/4 t. cayenne pepper
2 t. brown sugar, packed	1/4 t. nutmeg

Place chicken in an ungreased 13"x9" baking pan; set aside. Combine remaining ingredients in a small saucepan. Bring to a boil over medium-high heat; boil and stir for 2 minutes. Spoon mixture over chicken. Cover with aluminum foil; bake at 325 degrees for one hour. Uncover; baste chicken with pan drippings. Increase oven temperature to 450 degrees. Bake, uncovered, an additional 20 minutes, or until chicken is crisp and golden, about 20 more minutes. Serves 5.

Chicken thighs may be used in most recipes calling for chicken breasts. They're juicier, more flavorful and budget-friendly too.

Pork Chops with Old-Fashioned Gravy

Phyl Broich-Wessling
Garner, IA

Pork chops and gravy...simple but oh-so good!

3 T. all-purpose flour
1/2 t. seasoned salt
1/2 t. salt
4 bone-in pork chops,
    1-inch thick

2 T. shortening, melted
1-1/4 c. water, divided
5-oz. can evaporated milk

Combine flour and salt in a shallow dish. Dredge pork chops in flour mixture; reserve remaining mixture for gravy. In an oven-safe skillet over medium heat, brown chops in shortening on both sides. Add 1/2 cup water to skillet. Cover; bake at 350 degrees for 30 to 45 minutes, until tender. Add a little more water to skillet, if needed. Remove chops to a platter; keep warm. Drain skillet, reserving 2 tablespoons drippings. Stir in 2 tablespoons reserved flour mixture. Combine evaporated milk and 3/4 cup water; slowly add to skillet. Cook and stir over low heat until smooth and thickened. Serve gravy with chops. Serves 4.

For dark, rich-looking gravy, add a spoonful or two of brewed coffee.
It will add color to pale gravy but won't affect the flavor.

Sweet Pepper-Sausage Bake

*Lis McDonnell
New Castle, IN*

*This recipe became an instant family favorite. We love to use
fresh peppers and onions right out of the garden
during the summer months.*

3 T. olive oil, divided
14-oz. pkg. smoked pork
   sausage, sliced
3 to 4 potatoes, peeled
   and cubed

16-oz. pkg. mini sweet peppers,
   sliced
1 onion, sliced
salt and pepper to taste

Line a 13"x9" baking pan with aluminum foil. Brush one tablespoon
oil over foil; set aside. Combine sausage and vegetables in a large
bowl. Drizzle with remaining oil; mix to coat well and spread on pan.
Season with salt and pepper. Cover with another layer of foil, sealing
top and bottom of foil together. Bake at 350 degrees for 30 minutes,
or until vegetables are tender. Serves 3 to 4.

Smoked sausage links are a great choice for weeknight meals...
just brown and serve. Different flavors like hickory-smoked or
cheese-filled can really jazz up a recipe. Be sure to select
fully-cooked sausages, not the uncooked kind.

Unstuffed Peppers

Kay Macy
Plano, TX

My husband and I love stuffed peppers, but they take too much time to prepare. My kids don't like peppers but they love the stuffing. With this recipe, I can please everyone!

1-1/2 lbs. ground beef
1 onion, chopped
4 green peppers, halved and
    tops chopped
2 t. chili powder, or to taste
1 t. garlic powder
salt and pepper to taste

1 to 2 T. sugar
1 c. long-cooking rice, uncooked
15-oz. can tomato sauce
1-3/4 c. water
Optional: shredded Cheddar
    cheese

In a deep skillet over medium heat, brown beef with onion and chopped pepper tops. Drain; stir in seasonings and sugar. Add uncooked rice, tomato sauce and water. Bring to a boil. Reduce heat to low; cover and cook for 10 minutes, stirring occasionally. Add a little more water, if needed. Arrange pepper halves on top of beef mixture. Cover and cook until peppers are fork-tender, about 15 to 20 minutes, stirring gently but leaving the peppers on top. To serve, use a large spoon to place a pepper half on each plate; spoon in the filling. Peppers may be topped with cheese, if desired. Serves 6 to 8.

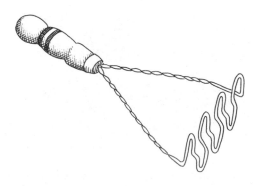

A clever way to crumble ground beef...use a potato masher right in the skillet.

Quick-Fix Chicken Pot Pie

Ashley Causey
Lumberton, TX

This batter-topped pot pie is super-quick to make,
since most of the ingredients are always kept on hand.
It has become one of our favorites.

1/2 c. plus 2 T. butter, divided
3 boneless skinless chicken
   breasts, cubed
1 t. garlic powder
1 t. onion powder
1/2 t. dried parsley
1 c. carrots, peeled and thinly
   sliced

1 c. frozen peas, thawed
10-3/4 oz. can cream of
   chicken soup
1 c. chicken broth
salt and pepper to taste
1-1/2 c. biscuit baking mix
1 c. milk

Melt 2 tablespoons butter in a skillet over medium heat; add chicken. Sprinkle chicken with seasonings; sauté until golden and juices run clear. Transfer chicken to a greased 2-quart casserole dish; layer with carrots and peas. In a small bowl, mix soup, broth, salt and pepper; pour over vegetables. In a separate bowl, stir together biscuit mix and milk; spoon over top. Melt remaining butter and drizzle over top. Bake, uncovered, at 350 degrees for 35 to 40 minutes, until topping is firm and golden. Serves 4.

Make mini pot pies. Spoon filling into oven-safe bowls and add batter topping, or cut circles of pie crust to fit, using another bowl as a guide. Set on a baking sheet and bake until bubbly and golden...delicious, and everyone gets their own little pot pie!

Beefy Shepherd's Pie

Kathryn Jones
Cheyenne, WY

As a young working mother, one day I was talking about not having anything planned for dinner when I got home that night. Thanks to my fellow engineer friend who gave me this recipe...it has been a life-saver for over 30 years now!

1 lb. lean ground beef
1/2 c. onion, chopped
1/3 c. catsup
1/3 c. mild salsa

1 c. frozen mixed vegetables
2 c. mashed potatoes
2 T. butter, sliced

Brown beef and onion in a skillet over medium heat. Drain; spread in a greased 8"x8" glass baking pan. Layer catsup, salsa and frozen vegetables over beef mixture. Cover with mashed potatoes; dot potatoes with pats of butter. Bake, uncovered, at 400 degrees for 30 to 40 minutes, until bubbly and golden. Serves 4.

Chicken & Broccoli Shepherd's Pie

Ann Hamerly
Snoqualmie, WA

My mom and grandma both made delicious shepherd's pies with leftovers. I learned to make my own with a new twist, and it turned out to be a family favorite!

4 c. cooked chicken, cubed
2 c. broccoli, cooked and
   chopped
10-3/4 oz. can cream of chicken
   soup

1/2 c. water
salt and pepper
2 to 3 c. mashed potatoes

In a bowl, combine chicken, broccoli, soup and water. Mix thoroughly; season with salt and pepper. Spread mixture in a greased 9" pie plate. Top with dollops of mashed potatoes. Bake, uncovered, at 350 degrees for 30 minutes, or until hot and bubbly. Makes 4 servings.

Barb's Skillet Lasagna

Robyn Binns
Crescent, IA

*Lasagna is the ultimate comfort food, but on busy nights
when you need some comfort and time is at a premium, this recipe
fits the bill...you don't even need to precook the noodles!*

1 lb. ground beef
1 onion, diced
26-oz. jar pasta sauce, divided
16-oz. container cottage cheese
8-oz. pkg. lasagna noodles,
    uncooked and broken in half

8-oz. pkg. shredded mozzarella
    cheese
Garnish: grated Parmesan
    cheese

In a large deep skillet over medium heat, brown beef and onion; drain.
Pour half of pasta sauce over beef; do not stir. Drop cottage cheese by
spoonfuls over sauce. Layer uncooked noodles over cottage cheese.
Spread with remaining sauce; do not stir. Cover and simmer over low
heat for 20 minutes. Check to see if there is a lot of liquid in the pan;
if so, leave uncovered and cook 15 minutes longer, or until noodles
are tender. If there isn't a lot of liquid, cover pan and cook 15 minutes
longer, or until noodles are tender. Sprinkle mozzarella cheese over
top; cover and remove from heat. Let stand 5 minutes. Top with
Parmesan cheese just before serving. Serves 6.

Place a bunch of fresh parsley in the fridge in a water-filled tumbler
covered with a plastic bag. It will keep its just-picked flavor
for up to a week.

Spaghetti & Meatballs

Naomi Townsend
Ozark, MO

This is my husband's favorite dish. He got the recipe from a friend in his hometown 25 years ago, and we've enjoyed it ever since. It has become a weekly event to serve spaghetti & meatballs, green salad and garlic bread...yummy! Leftovers are great too.

2 8-oz. cans tomato sauce,
   divided
1.4-oz. pkg. French onion
   soup mix
1 c. water
1 lb. ground beef

1 t. dried parsley
1/2 t. dried thyme
1/2 t. garlic salt
1/4 t. pepper
6-oz. can tomato paste
cooked spaghetti

In a saucepan over medium heat, stir together 1-1/2 cans tomato sauce, soup mix and water; cover and bring to a boil. Reduce heat to low; simmer for 15 minutes, stirring occasionally. Meanwhile, combine beef, remaining tomato sauce and seasonings in a bowl. Blend well with your hands; form into one-inch meatballs. Add meatballs to sauce, one at a time, making sure all meatballs are covered with sauce. Simmer, uncovered, for 30 minutes, stirring occasionally. Stir in tomato paste; simmer for another 30 minutes. Serve meatballs and sauce over cooked spaghetti. Makes 4 servings.

Dip your hands into cold water before shaping meatballs...
the meat won't stick to your hands.

Church Chicken

Cyndy DeStefano
Mercer, PA

When I was growing up, Sunday was always my favorite day. We would come home from church to the aroma of something wonderful cooking in the oven. After dinner, the rest of the day was dedicated to visiting with extended family, playing games and watching "Wonderful World of Disney" on TV. Every time I make this recipe, I remember those simpler times.

3-1/2 to 4-lb. roasting chicken	poultry seasoning, garlic
2 lemons, halved and divided	powder, salt and pepper
2 onions, quartered and divided	to taste
4 stalks celery, divided	

Place chicken in a roasting pan sprayed with butter-flavored non-stick vegetable spray. Place 2 lemon halves, 4 onion quarters and 2 celery stalks inside chicken. Squeeze remaining lemon halves over chicken and add lemon halves to pan; arrange remaining onion and celery around chicken. Spray chicken generously with butter-flavored spray; sprinkle with seasonings. Bake, uncovered, at 350 degrees for about 2-1/2 hours, basting chicken twice with pan juices as it bakes. Chicken is done when a meat thermometer inserted in thickest part of chicken reads 165 degrees and chicken juices run clear. Remove chicken to a platter; discard vegetables. Let stand for 5 to 10 minutes before carving. Serves 4.

A large roasting pan can handle plenty of kitchen tasks besides roasting chicken, turkey and pot roasts. It's also terrific for oven-browning batches of meatballs, stirring up lots of snack mix... even set it over two stovetop burners and boil sweet corn for a crowd!

No-Peek Chicken & Rice

Jennie Gist
Gooseberry Patch

*This recipe came from my late Aunt Dorothy. It's such
a simple recipe, yet so elegant when served with
steamed asparagus and buttered hot rolls.*

10-3/4 oz. can cream of
    mushroom soup
10-3/4 oz. can cream of celery
    soup
6-oz. pkg. long grain & wild rice
    mix, uncooked

1-1/4 c. water
1 t. dried parsley
1/8 t. curry powder
4 chicken breasts, or 8 chicken
    thighs and drumsticks
1.35-oz. pkg. onion soup mix

In a large bowl, mix soups, rice mix, seasoning packet from rice, water,
parsley and curry powder. Spoon into a lightly greased 13"x9" baking
pan. Remove skin from chicken, if desired. Arrange chicken on top of
rice mixture; sprinkle soup mix over chicken. Cover tightly with
aluminum foil. Bake at 350 degrees for 2-1/2 hours, or until rice is
tender and chicken juices run clear when pierced. Serves 4.

Oh-so-easy iced tea...perfect with dinner anytime. Fill a two-quart pitcher
with water and drop in six to eight tea bags. Refrigerate overnight.
Discard tea bags; add sugar to taste and serve over ice.

Brown Sugar Meatloaf

Misty Raines
Cumberland, MD

As a recent newlywed, I was taken aback by how much my husband could eat...he's 6'4" and I'm only 5'2"! So I started searching for recipes that were both hearty and tasty. This one is his favorite. It goes very well with homemade mac & cheese, fresh green beans and a pitcher of sweet tea.

1/2 c. catsup	1-1/2 t. salt
1/2 c. brown sugar, packed	1/4 t. pepper
1 lb. ground beef	1 onion, chopped
3/4 c. milk	3/4 c. saltine crackers, crushed
2 eggs, beaten	1 t. Worcestershire sauce

Mix together catsup and brown sugar in a small bowl; set aside. In a large bowl, combine remaining ingredients; mix by hand and form into a loaf. Place in a lightly greased 9"x5" loaf pan. Spoon catsup mixture over meatloaf. Bake, uncovered, at 350 degrees for one hour. Serves 8.

Post a dinner wish list on the fridge and invite everyone to jot down their favorite dishes. Family members who are involved in meal planning are much more likely to look forward to family dinnertime together!

Mini Cheddar Meatloaves

Krissy Darrington
Declo, ID

My husband and children love these yummy mini loaves! He tells me all the time that he'd ask for this as his last meal. My six-year-old daughter will eat three of these, even though one is more than enough for me. I have shared this recipe over & over again.

3/4 c. milk
1 egg
1 t. salt
1 c. shredded Cheddar cheese
1/2 c. quick-cooking oats,
    uncooked

1/2 c. onion, chopped
1 lb. ground beef
2/3 c. catsup
1/2 c. brown sugar, packed
Optional: mustard to taste

In a large bowl, whisk milk, egg and salt with a fork. Add cheese, oats, onion and beef. Mix by hand; form into 10 small meatloaves. Place meatloaves in a lightly greased 13"x9" baking pan. In a small bowl, mix catsup, brown sugar and a small amount of mustard, if desired. Spoon evenly over meatloaves. Cover with aluminum foil. Bake at 350 degrees for 30 to 45 minutes, until juices run clear. Serves 5.

Cut leftover meatloaf into thick slices, wrap individually and freeze.
Slices can be thawed and rewarmed quickly for scrumptious
meatloaf sandwiches at a moment's notice.

Chicken & Spaghetti Casserole

Nadine Rush
London, KY

Our church's hot food ministry cooks and delivers dinner to 50 people every Friday evening. This is the recipe I fix whenever we've decided on a spaghetti casserole...it feeds a crowd, yet it's not difficult to make. My daughters love it too.

5 to 6 boneless, skinless chicken breasts
2 to 3 stalks celery, diced
1 onion, diced
salt and pepper to taste
16-oz. pkg. spaghetti, uncooked and broken in half

2 10-3/4 oz. cans cream of chicken soup
8 slices pasteurized process cheese spread
10-oz. pkg. shredded mozzarella cheese

In a large soup pot, combine chicken, celery, onion, salt and pepper; cover with water. Bring to a boil over medium-high heat. Reduce heat to low; simmer until chicken is tender, 30 to 45 minutes. Remove chicken to a plate, reserving broth, celery and onion in soup pot. Bring broth to a boil. Add spaghetti and cook until tender, 8 to 10 minutes; drain. Meanwhile, shred chicken. Combine chicken and soup in a large bowl; transfer to a greased deep 13"x9" glass baking pan. Spoon spaghetti mixture over chicken mixture. Arrange cheese slices on top; sprinkle with shredded cheese. Bake, uncovered, at 350 degrees for 25 minutes, or just until cheese melts and turns golden. Serves 12.

Perfect pasta! Fill a large pot with water and bring to a rolling boil.
Add a tablespoon of salt, if desired. Stir in pasta; return to a rolling boil.
Boil, uncovered, for the time suggested on package. There's no need to
add oil...frequent stirring will keep pasta from sticking together.

Meatless Spaghetti Pie

Vickie

An old standby that everyone likes! Beef it up with browned ground beef, or add some pepperoni and mushrooms to make it a pizza pie.

7-oz. pkg. spaghetti, uncooked
1 c. cottage cheese
3 eggs, divided
1-1/2 t. salt
1/8 t. pepper

1 c. shredded sharp Cheddar
   cheese
2 T. grated Parmesan cheese
Garnish: warm pasta sauce

Cook spaghetti according to package directions; drain. In a bowl, gently mix spaghetti, cottage cheese, 2 beaten eggs, salt, pepper and Cheddar cheese. Transfer to a greased 9" deep-dish pie plate. Beat together remaining egg and Parmesan cheese; spread over top. Bake, uncovered, at 350 degrees for 45 to 55 minutes, until a knife tip inserted in the center comes out clean. Cut into wedges; spoon some sauce over each wedge. Serves 6 to 8.

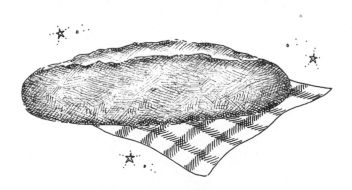

Whip up some savory garlic bread...yum! Split a loaf of Italian bread. Broil cut-side up until golden, 3 to 4 minutes. Meanwhile, blend 2 tablespoons softened butter, 2 tablespoons olive oil and 2 teaspoons minced garlic. Spread butter mixture over hot bread; sprinkle with Parmesan cheese. Return to broiler for about 30 seconds, until crisp.

Hurry-Up Italian Casserole

Narita Roady
Pryor, OK

I'm always looking for ways to serve dinner in a hurry and also trying to get more vegetables into our diet. This dish does both!

4 zucchini, thinly sliced
1/2 c. water
1 lb. ground beef
1/2 c. onion, chopped
2 cloves garlic, minced
1-1/2 t. Italian seasoning

1/2 t. salt
1 T. olive oil
2 c. fresh spinach, torn
1-1/2 c. marinara sauce
1-1/2 c. shredded mozzarella
cheese

Place zucchini and water in a saucepan over medium heat. Cook until tender, about 5 minutes; drain. Meanwhile, in a skillet over medium heat, brown beef, onion and garlic. Drain; sprinkle with seasonings. Spoon into a 9"x9" glass baking pan and set aside. Add oil to same skillet; add spinach and stir until wilted. Combine spinach and zucchini; mix well and spread over beef mixture. Spread marinara sauce over top; sprinkle with cheese. Bake, uncovered, at 350 degrees for 20 minutes, or until bubbly and cheese is melted. Makes 6 servings.

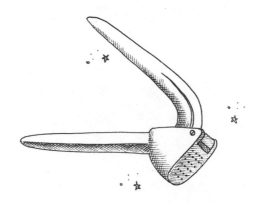

Save chopping time...use a garlic press. Don't even bother peeling the clove, just place it in the garlic press and close. The peel slides right off and the paste is easily removed for any recipe.

Baked Macaroni & Eggplant

JoAnn

*If you like Eggplant Parmesan, you'll love this cheesy version
with the pasta baked right in.*

8-oz. pkg. ziti pasta, uncooked
2 to 3 T. olive oil
1 eggplant, peeled and thinly
   sliced
26-oz. jar pasta sauce, divided

8-oz. pkg. shredded mozzarella
   cheese, divided
6 T. grated Parmesan cheese,
   divided

Cook pasta as package directs; drain. Meanwhile, heat oil in a large
skillet over medium heat. Cook eggplant slices in oil, a few slices at a
time, until golden on both sides. Drain eggplant on paper towels; keep
warm. Combine pasta and sauce, reserving one cup sauce for top of
casserole. In a lightly greased 2-quart casserole dish, layer half the
pasta mixture, 3/4 cup mozzarella cheese, half the eggplant and
2 tablespoons Parmesan cheese; repeat layers. Top with reserved
sauce and remaining cheeses. Bake, uncovered, at 425 degrees for
15 minutes, or until hot and bubbly. Serves 4 to 6.

Aged Parmesan cheese is most flavorful when it's freshly grated.
A chunk of Parmesan will stay fresh in the fridge for several weeks
if wrapped in a paper towel dampened with cider vinegar
and then tucked into a plastic zipping bag.

Best Oven-Fried Chicken Ever

Kristin Santangelo-Winterhoff
North Chili, NY

I first taste-tested this amazing recipe at my mother's house. I was a bit skeptical, but this is the most delicious oven-baked "fried" chicken you will ever taste!

1 c. butter, melted and divided
2 cloves garlic, pressed
8 to 10 slices white bread
1/3 c. grated Parmesan cheese
2 T. fresh parsley, chopped
1 t. salt
1/8 t. pepper
3-1/2 lbs. chicken, cut up

In a shallow dish, combine butter and garlic; set aside. Process bread slices into crumbs in a food processor; place in a shallow dish. Add cheese, parsley, salt and pepper to crumbs. Dip chicken pieces into butter mixture, then into crumb mixture. Reserve any remaining butter mixture. Arrange chicken in an ungreased shallow 13"x9" baking pan. Drizzle remaining butter over chicken. Bake, covered, at 350 degrees for one to 1-1/4 hours, turning several times, until chicken juices run clear when pierced. Serves 4 to 6.

Even a simple supper can be memorable when it's thoughtfully served.
Use the good china, set out cloth napkins and a jar of fresh flowers...
after all, who's more special than your family?

Pork Chop Skillet Supper

Barbara Cebula
Chicopee, MA

My tried & true recipe for a busy-day supper...my family loves it!

1/2 c. all-purpose flour
6 bone-in pork loin chops,
   3/4-inch thick
2 T. olive oil
2 t. dried thyme
2 t. salt
1/4 t. pepper

4 to 5 potatoes, peeled and cut
   into 3/4-inch cubes
5 carrots, peeled and sliced
   1/4 inch thick
1 onion, cut into wedges
3 c. beef broth

Place flour in a large resealable plastic zipping bag. Add pork chops to bag, a few at a time; shake to coat. Heat oil in a large skillet over medium heat; brown pork chops on both sides. Drain; season with thyme, salt and pepper. Add vegetables to skillet. Pour broth into skillet; bring to a boil. Reduce heat to medium-low; cover and simmer for 40 to 50 minutes, until pork chops are no longer pink inside and vegetables are tender. Makes 6 servings.

Make your own dry bread crumbs...a terrific way to use day-old bread.
Dry out bread slices in a 250-degree oven, then tear into
sections and pulse in your food processor or blender.

Taco Hot Bake

KellyJean Gettelfinger
Sellersburg, IN

*This recipe is fun because everyone can garnish their portion
just the way they like! Try using nacho cheese tortilla chips or
plain corn chips instead of chili cheese corn chips too.*

2 lbs. ground beef
2 1-1/4 oz. pkgs. taco
   seasoning mix
1-1/3 c. water
6-oz. pkg. chili cheese corn
   chips
2 10-3/4 oz. cans Cheddar
   cheese soup

1 c. milk
16-oz. pkg. shredded mozzarella
   cheese, divided
Toppings: sour cream, shredded
   lettuce, halved cherry
   tomatoes, sliced black olives,
   sliced mushrooms

Brown beef in a large skillet over medium heat; drain. Stir in taco
seasoning and water; bring to a boil. Reduce heat to low; simmer for
5 minutes, stirring occasionally. Spread corn chips evenly in a lightly
greased 13"x9" baking pan. Spoon beef mixture over chips; set aside.
In a saucepan over medium-low heat, stir soup and milk until smooth
and heated through. Spoon soup mixture over beef mixture. Top with
3 cups cheese. Bake, uncovered, at 350 degrees for 10 to 15 minutes,
until hot and bubbly. Remove from oven; top with remaining cheese.
Garnish individual portions with desired toppings. Serves 6 to 8.

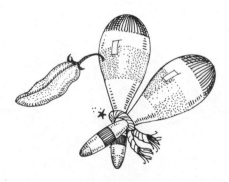

Cutting back? Try using a little less ground beef in tried & true recipes
like Taco Hot Bake. Add a few more veggies and toppings...
chances are good that no one will even notice!

Chicken Stacks

Jennifer Rubino
Hickory, NC

When my children were little, every time they liked what I cooked, they asked me, "Is this a Gooseberry Patch recipe?" They knew that all my good recipes were from my many Gooseberry cookbooks. Imagine my delight when my now-teenagers tasted this original recipe of mine and said, "You need to send this recipe to Gooseberry Patch!" So here it is...I hope you love it too!

8 8-inch burrito-size flour
   tortillas
16-oz. can refried beans
19-oz. can enchilada sauce
2 12-1/2 oz. cans white
   chicken, drained and flaked

1-1/2 c. sharp shredded Cheddar
   cheese
Optional: shredded lettuce,
   corn kernels, diced tomatoes,
   sour cream

Spray a 2-quart round casserole dish with non-stick vegetable spray; set aside. Heat beans in a saucepan over medium-low heat. Heat enchilada sauce in a separate saucepan over medium heat. Add chicken to sauce. Place one tortilla in the bottom of casserole dish; layer with beans, cheese and a ladle of sauce mixture. Add another tortilla; repeat layering with remaining ingredients, ending with a tortilla on top. Sprinkle with cheese. Bake, uncovered, at 350 degrees for 15 minutes, or until hot and bubbly. Let stand 5 to 10 minutes; cut into wedges. Serve topped with desired toppings. Makes 6 to 8 servings.

A savory roast chicken from the deli is the busy cook's secret ingredient! The chicken is already cooked and ready for whatever recipe you decide to make...just slice, chop or shred as needed.

Chicken & Parsley Dumplings

Kathleen Kennedy
Renton, WA

This is my go-to dish when the family is gathered together in the fall and winter. I've been making this dinner over 30 years, so you know it's tried & true!

4 to 5-lb. stewing chicken,
   cut up
2 carrots, peeled and sliced
1 onion, sliced
1 stalk celery, sliced
1 t. salt
1 c. milk
1/3 c. all-purpose flour

In a stockpot, cover chicken pieces with water; add vegetables and salt. Bring to a boil over high heat; reduce heat to low. Cover and simmer for 2-1/2 to 3 hours, until chicken is very tender; do not boil. Remove chicken and vegetables to a large bowl, reserving broth. Discard bones and skin from chicken; keep chicken and vegetables warm. Strain broth and measure; add enough water to equal 3 cups. Return broth to pan along with chicken and vegetables; bring to a boil. Combine milk and flour in a covered jar; shake until smooth. Add slowly to broth, stirring with a whisk. Drop dough for Parsley Dumplings into broth by tablespoonfuls. Simmer, uncovered, for 10 minutes. Cover; simmer another 10 minutes. Serves 4 to 6.

Parsley Dumplings:

2 c. all-purpose flour
1 T. baking powder
1 t. salt
1/4 c. fresh parsley, chopped
1/4 c. shortening
1 c. milk

Stir together flour, baking powder and salt; add parsley. Cut in shortening with a fork until mixture resembles cornmeal. Stir in milk until a soft dough forms.

Freeze extra homemade chicken broth in ice cube trays for down-home flavor when cooking rice, pasta or potatoes.

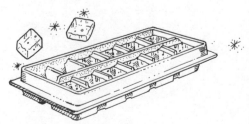

Newlywed Roast

Charlene McCain
Bakersfield, CA

Every new bride needs a can't-fail dish, and this is mine...that's why I call it the Newlywed Roast. Simple to prepare, yet delicious enough for the fussiest mother-in-law! I have served it to company for years, and it still gets raves.

1 T. oil
3-lb. beef chuck roast, rump
    roast or 7-bone roast
1/2 c. all-purpose flour
10-3/4 oz. can cream of
    mushroom soup

1.35-oz. pkg. onion soup mix
1 c. water
8 potatoes, halved or quartered
6 carrots, peeled and chopped
1 onion, quartered

Place oil in a Dutch oven or other heavy oven-safe pot with a lid. Heat over medium heat. Roll roast in flour until it is coated on all sides. Place roast in hot oil and brown on all sides. Remove from heat. In a bowl, mix together soup, soup mix and water. Pour mixture over roast. Cover pot with lid. Bake at 325 degrees for 3 hours. Remove from oven; arrange vegetables around roast. Return to oven for another 30 minutes, or until vegetables are tender. Transfer roast to a platter; surround with vegetables. Let roast stand for several minutes before slicing. Makes 8 servings.

For best results when browning a roast, use a heavy pan...cast iron is ideal. Heat the pan over medium-high heat for one to 2 minutes before adding the oil. Let the oil warm, then add your roast and cook on all sides, turning only occasionally until roast is well browned.

Sausage & Sauerkraut Skillet

Charlotte Smith
Tyrone, PA

This is a quick and tasty meal. There are never any leftovers!

4 potatoes, peeled and cubed
2 T. oil
1 onion, halved and sliced
1 lb. smoked pork sausage link,
    sliced 1/4-inch thick

16-oz. pkg. sauerkraut, rinsed
    and well drained
1/8 t. salt
1/8 t. pepper

In a large skillet over medium heat, sauté potatoes in oil for 5 to
6 minutes, until lightly golden. Stir in onion; sauté for 4 to 5 minutes,
until tender. Add sausage and sauerkraut to skillet; season with salt
and pepper. Simmer, uncovered, for about 10 minutes, stirring
occasionally, until heated through. Makes 4 servings.

Decorate vintage clip clothespins by gluing on scraps of
pretty scrapbooking paper. Add a button magnet on the back...
handy for holding shopping lists, recipe cards and school
photos on the refrigerator.

Oven-Barbecued Ribs

Katie Cooper
Chubbuck, ID

A good friend gave me this easy, tasty recipe...try it, you'll like it too!

3 to 4 lbs. boneless pork ribs
salt to taste
1 lemon, thinly sliced
1 onion, thinly sliced
1 c. catsup

1-1/2 c. water
1/3 c. Worcestershire sauce
1/4 t. hot pepper sauce
1 t. salt

Season ribs with salt; arrange in a shallow roasting pan. Bake, uncovered, at 450 degrees for 30 minutes. Drain fat from pan. Top each rib with a slice of lemon and onion. Combine remaining ingredients in a bowl. Reduce oven temperature to 350 degrees. Cover and bake until well done, about 1-1/2 hours, basting ribs with catsup mixture every 15 minutes. Serves 4 to 6.

Family-Favorite Pork Chops

Shelly Dushek
Owatonna, MN

My mom made this recipe for our family when I was growing up.
Now I make it for my family...there are never any leftovers!

8 bone-in pork chops,
   3/4-inch thick
8 t. lemon juice

1/2 c. brown sugar, packed
1/2 c. onion, chopped
1 c. catsup

Arrange pork chops in a lightly greased 13"x9" baking pan, overlapping if necessary. In the order given, top each pork chop with one teaspoon lemon juice, one tablespoon brown sugar, one tablespoon onion and 2 tablespoons catsup. Add a small amount of water to cover bottom of pan. Cover with aluminum foil. Bake at 375 degrees for one hour. Remove foil; bake an additional 30 minutes. Makes 8 servings.

Baked Tilapia & Peppers

Marybeth Hunton
Jefferson City, MO

My family has always enjoyed fried fish, so I was pleasantly surprised when they liked this baked fish dish. My husband isn't fond of any type of bell peppers...he likes the fish baked with them, he just doesn't eat the peppers!

1 lemon
salt and pepper to taste
4 tilapia fillets
1 green pepper, cut in strips

1 red pepper, cut in strips
1 yellow pepper, cut in strips
1/2 c. white wine or water
2 to 3 t. olive oil

Grate zest from lemon. Mix zest with salt and pepper in a small bowl; set aside. Cover a 15"x10" jelly-roll pan with aluminum foil. Grease lightly; place peppers on foil. Cut lemon in half; squeeze 1/4 cup juice from lemon. Drizzle peppers with wine or water, lemon juice and olive oil. Sprinkle with salt and pepper; toss gently. Arrange fish fillets on top; sprinkle fish with lemon zest mixture. Slice lemon halves very thinly; top each fillet with 2 to 3 lemon slices. Fold up foil and seal tightly. Bake at 350 degrees for 20 minutes, or until fish flakes easily with a fork. Makes 4 servings.

Stem and seed a green pepper in a flash...hold the pepper upright on a cutting board. Use a sharp knife to slice each of the sides from the pepper. You'll then have four large seedless pieces ready for slicing or chopping.

Comfort-Food Main Dishes

Maple Syrup Salmon

Brandi Thomas
Saint Cloud, FL

I never cared much for fish until I tried this recipe. The sweet taste of the salmon melts in your mouth. Delicious!

1 c. butter, melted
4 6-oz. salmon fillets,
   skin removed
4 t. salt

4 t. pepper
4 t. granulated onion
4 t. granulated garlic
1 c. maple syrup, warmed

Brush melted butter over top and sides of salmon fillets; brush remaining butter over a baking sheet. Arrange fillets on baking sheet. Sprinkle with seasonings, gently pressing them in. Bake, uncovered, at 350 degrees for 25 to 30 minutes, just until golden. Drizzle fillets with maple syrup about 10 minutes before removing from oven. Makes 4 servings.

Baked Lemon Pepper Fish

Sue Klapper
Muskego, WI

A fine last-minute dinner...you don't even have to thaw the fish!

12-oz. pkg. frozen cod or
   tilapia fillets
1/4 t. lemon pepper
1/4 t. dried basil

1 tomato, sliced
2 T. green onion, sliced
2 T. grated Parmesan cheese

Arrange frozen fish fillets in a lightly greased 8"x8" baking pan. Sprinkle with lemon pepper and basil. Bake, uncovered, at 375 degrees for 15 minutes. Top each fillet with a tomato slice; sprinkle with onion and cheese. Return to oven for an additional 10 minutes, or just until fish flakes easily with a fork. Serves 4.

Chicken Piccata

Eugenia Taylor
Stroudsburg, PA

I found this recipe tucked in the back of a book that my mom was reading. It is a great go-to dinner.

1/2 c. boiling water
2 cubes chicken bouillon
3 T. lemon juice, divided
1 egg
4 boneless, skinless chicken
  breasts

1/4 c. all-purpose flour
1/8 t. garlic powder
1/8 t. paprika
1/4 c. butter, sliced
cooked rice

Combine boiling water, bouillon cubes and 2 tablespoons lemon juice in a cup; set aside. In a shallow dish, beat egg with remaining lemon juice. In a separate shallow dish, combine flour, garlic powder and paprika. Dip chicken into egg mixture, then into flour mixture. Melt butter in a large skillet over medium-high heat. Cook chicken until golden on both sides. Stir bouillon mixture; add to skillet. Reduce heat to medium-low. Cover and simmer for 20 minutes, or until chicken juices run clear when pierced. Serve chicken and pan sauce over rice. Makes 4 servings.

Boneless chicken breasts cook up quickly and evenly when flattened.
Simply place chicken between two pieces of plastic wrap and gently
pound to desired thickness with a meat mallet or a small skillet.

Chicken Parmesan

Jessalyn Wantland
Napoleon, OH

Just six ingredients, but so yummy! Jazz it up with your favorite flavor of pasta sauce...there are plenty to choose from.

1 egg, beaten
3/4 c. Italian-seasoned dry
   bread crumbs
4 boneless, skinless chicken
   breasts

26-oz. jar pasta sauce
1 c. shredded mozzarella cheese
cooked spaghetti

Place egg and bread crumbs in separate shallow dishes. Dip chicken in egg, then in bread crumbs. Place in a greased 13"x9" baking pan. Bake, uncovered, at 400 degrees for 30 minutes. Spoon pasta sauce over chicken and top with cheese. Bake another 15 minutes, or until chicken juices run clear. Serve chicken and sauce over spaghetti. Makes 4 servings.

Those Chicken Breasts

Judy Taylor
Butler, MO

Both of my grown kids still love this family favorite and request it for their birthday dinners. I know what they'll say when I ask what they want...their reply is always "Those chicken breasts!"

4 boneless, skinless chicken
   breasts
3/4 c. milk
1 egg, beaten
salt and pepper to taste

1 sleeve saltine crackers, finely
   crushed
shortening or oil for frying
6 slices white bread

Pound chicken breasts well to flatten. Beat together milk, egg, salt and pepper in a shallow dish; place cracker crumbs in a separate dish. Dip chicken into egg mixture, then into cracker crumbs. Heat 3/4-inch depth shortening or oil in a skillet over medium heat. Cook chicken until golden on both sides. Line a baking sheet with bread slices. Place chicken on the bread to absorb excess grease. Bake, uncovered, at 350 degrees for 15 to 20 minutes, until chicken juices run clear. Serve bread with chicken or discard. Serves 4.

Saucy Almond-Chicken Stir-Fry

Sue Klapper
Muskego, WI

We just love the way this tangy sauce smothers the rice.
The crunch of the almonds and water chestnuts makes a
delightful contrast. Enjoy...we do!

3 c. instant brown rice,
   uncooked
2-1/2 c. water
1 T. sesame oil
1 t. garlic, minced
4 boneless, skinless
   chicken breasts, cut
   into 1-inch cubes

1/2 c. slivered almonds
1 red pepper, cut into 3/4" strips
2 9-oz. pkgs. frozen sugar
   snap peas
8-oz. can sliced water chestnuts,
   drained

Prepare rice with water according to package directions. Meanwhile, heat oil and garlic in a large skillet or wok over medium-high heat. Add chicken and almonds. Cook for 5 minutes, stirring often, until chicken and almonds are golden. Add remaining ingredients; cook and stir for 3 to 4 minutes. Pour Stir-Fry Sauce into skillet; cook and stir until thick and bubbly. Serve over cooked rice. Serves 6 to 8.

Stir-Fry Sauce:

14-1/2 oz. chicken broth
1/4 c. low-sodium soy sauce
2 T. cider vinegar

1/4 c. cornstarch
1 T. sugar

Stir together all ingredients in a bowl; stir again just before using.

Laughter is the best dinnertime music.
   – Carleton Kendrick

Baked Pork Chop Suey

Evelyn Hammen
Little Chute, WI

One of my most-requested recipes...it never fails me! When my son-in-law was visiting for dinner, he had three helpings and just raved about it. My friend, who is blind and quite a cook himself, always wants me to make it for him too.

2 T. oil
5 T. soy sauce
2 lbs. boneless pork steaks,
    cut into bite-size cubes
4-oz. can sliced mushrooms
10-3/4 oz. can cream of
    mushroom soup
10-3/4 oz. can chicken & rice
    soup
8-oz. can sliced water chestnuts,
    drained

14-oz. can bean sprouts, drained
2 c. celery, diced
1 onion, chopped
2-2/3 c. water
1 T. browning and seasoning
    sauce
1 t. salt
1/2 t. pepper
cooked rice
Garnish: chow mein noodles

Heat oil and soy sauce in a deep skillet over medium heat. Brown pork on all sides. Transfer pork mixture to an ungreased 13"x9" baking pan. Add undrained mushrooms and remaining ingredients except rice and garnish; mix well. Bake, covered, at 350 degrees for 1-1/2 hours. Serve over cooked rice, topped with chow mein noodles. Serves 8.

Casseroles spell comfort food, but what if the recipe is large and your family is small? Simple...just divide the casserole ingredients into two small dishes and freeze one for later!

Farmstand Stir-Fry

Grace Smith
Vancouver, British Columbia

A veggie-packed dish to cook up in just a few minutes. Serve it over cooked rice or thin spaghetti, or enjoy as a side dish.

2 T. butter
2 T. oil
2 t. chicken bouillon granules
1 clove garlic, minced
1 lb. zucchini, thinly sliced

1/2 lb. sliced mushrooms
1 red pepper, diced
4 green onions, sliced
zest and juice of 1/2 lemon

In a skillet over medium heat, combine butter, oil, bouillon and garlic. Cook and stir until butter melts and bouillon dissolves. Increase heat to medium-high. Add zucchini and mushrooms; cook and stir for 3 to 5 minutes. Add red pepper and green onions; cook and stir for another 2 to 4 minutes, until vegetables are crisp-tender. Stir in lemon zest and juice; serve immediately. Makes 6 servings.

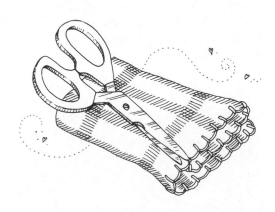

Kitchen shears are so handy! You'll find yourself using them again & again for snipping fresh herbs, cutting green onions, chopping canned tomatoes right in the can and opening packages. Just remember to wash them with soap and water after each use.

Broccoli & Ricotta-Stuffed Shells

Crystal Inestroza
Athens, AL

Any leftover Alfredo sauce may be spooned over grilled chicken breasts, which go well with this dish.

12-oz. pkg. jumbo pasta shells,
   uncooked
16-oz. container ricotta cheese
1/4 c. shredded Parmesan
   cheese
1 egg, beaten
1 T. garlic, minced

1 t. Italian seasoning
1/4 t. pepper
10-oz. pkg. frozen chopped
   broccoli, thawed and well
   drained
2 15-oz. jars Alfredo sauce
1 c. water

Cook pasta according to package directions. Drain and rinse with cold water. Meanwhile, in a bowl, mix remaining ingredients except sauce and water. Stuff each shell with one tablespoon of ricotta mixture. Arrange shells in a lightly greased 13"x9" baking pan; set aside. Combine sauce and water in a saucepan; heat over medium-low heat until warmed through. Ladle sauce over shells, covering all shells with sauce. Reserve any remaining sauce for another use. Cover pan with aluminum foil. Bake at 350 degrees for 40 to 45 minutes, until hot and bubbly. Serves 6.

No-mess stuffed pasta shells! Spoon cheese filling into a plastic zipping bag. Clip off a corner of the bag and squeeze the filling into shells, then toss away the bag.

Oh-So-Easy Shredded Chicken

Beth Richter
Canby, MN

I started using this slow-cooker recipe several years ago when I wanted a no-fuss weeknight meal. Now it's one of my most-requested dishes. We use it often for reunions and parties too. For a different flavor, use Mexican or mesquite BBQ seasoning mix instead of the ranch dressing mix.

3 lbs. boneless, skinless chicken breasts and/or thighs
1-oz. pkg. ranch salad dressing mix

1/2 to 1 c. chicken broth

Arrange chicken pieces in a 6-quart slow cooker, overlapping as necessary. Sprinkle dressing mix over chicken. Pour in broth until chicken is almost but not quite covered. Cover and cook on low setting for 6 to 8 hours, stirring after 5 to 6 hours, until chicken can easily be shredded. Serve chicken as desired. Serves 10 to 12.

Variations:

Shredded chicken may be served in sandwiches, wraps, quesadillas, casseroles, gravies or salads.

Shredded chicken, pork and beef sandwiches are real crowd-pleasers...
and with a slow cooker, they're a snap to fix. Serve them on busy
family nights or tote them to potlucks right in the crock.

Versatile Shredded Pork

Carly St. Clair
Lynnwood, WA

This slow-cooker recipe is really handy. Serve it right from the crock, paired with warm tortillas, refried beans & rice, or as the tasty start of lots of other dishes.

4-lb. pork blade or picnic
   shoulder roast
1 T. browning & seasoning
   sauce

1.35-oz. pkg onion soup mix
5 green chiles, halved, seeded
   and diced
1/2 c. water

Rub roast all over with browning sauce; sprinkle with soup mix all over the roast. Place roast fat-side up in a 6-quart slow cooker coated with non-stick vegetable spray. Spoon chiles over roast. Pour water around roast. Cover and cook on low setting for 6 to 8 hours, until roast is very tender. Shred roast with 2 forks. Serve shredded pork as desired. Serves 10.

Variations:

Shredded pork may be used to make tacos, burritos, tostadas, taco salads, sandwich buns or Sloppy Joes.

Make sure to use the right-size slow cooker...they work best when at least half of the crock is filled. A 5-1/2 to 6-quart slow cooker is ideal for most families.

Never-Fail Beef Stew

Shirl Parsons
Cape Carteret, NC

This tried & true recipe is a mainstay for my family, handed down from my mom and her mom. During the cold Canadian winters, Mom made this stew weekly. Sure to be a hit with your family too!

1 c. all-purpose flour
1 to 2 lbs. stew beef cubes
2 to 3 T. oil
4 to 5 potatoes, peeled and
  quartered
1 to 2 carrots, peeled and cut
  into chunks

1 onion, sliced
1/2 t. salt
1/8 t. pepper
14-1/2 oz. can whole tomatoes,
  or 2 c. cocktail vegetable
  juice
1/2 c. water

Place flour in a plastic zipping bag; add beef and toss to coat. Heat oil in a skillet over medium-high heat. Lightly brown beef on all sides; drain. Layer all ingredients in a 6-quart slow cooker in the order listed. Do not stir. Cover and cook on low setting for 8 to 9 hours, or on high setting for 4 hours, until beef and vegetables are tender. Stir gently before serving. Serves 6.

Long, slow cooking is ideal for inexpensive cuts of meat because it provides plenty of time for tenderizing. Meat turns out juicy and delicious...budget-friendly too.

Chicken & Dumplings

Lynne Carey
Bowling Green, KY

We love the chicken & dumplings at a favorite country-style restaurant, but I wanted to find a simple way to make them at home. Now my dad asks for these at least once a month. It has become his comfort food as his health fails.

2 lbs. boneless, skinless
   chicken tenderloins
26-oz. can cream of chicken
   soup
10-3/4 oz. can cream of
   chicken soup

pepper to taste
1-1/2 c. water, divided
12-oz. tube refrigerated flaky
   biscuits

Place chicken in a 6-quart slow cooker. In a bowl, blend soup, pepper and one cup water; spoon over chicken. Cover and cook on low setting for 4 hours, or until chicken shreds easily. Shred chicken in crock with 2 forks; add remaining water and stir well. Increase to high setting; cover and cook for 30 minutes. Tear biscuits into quarters; add to slow cooker and gently stir down. Cover and cook on high setting for an additional 30 minutes, or until dumplings are done. Makes 4 to 6 servings.

Variation:

Chicken Stew: Cook and shred chicken as directed above; stir in one cup water. Omit biscuits. For final step, stir in one 8-ounce package wide egg noodles and one 15-ounce can of peas & carrots, drained. Increase final cook time on high setting to one hour, or until noodles are tender.

To make clean-up a breeze, lightly spray the inside of a slow cooker with non-stick vegetable spray before adding recipe ingredients. What a time-saver!

Foolproof Pot Roast 3 Ways

Deanna Adams
Garland, TX

I experimented with my mother's traditional pot roast recipe for years before I got it just the way I wanted it. Then I started using my slow cooker, and it turned into more of a formula with variations. A pork loin cooked this way is also very good.

3 to 4 t. salt
1-1/2 to 2 t. pepper
1-1/2 to 2 t. garlic powder
3 to 4-lb. lean beef chuck roast
  or top round roast
1 lb. baby carrots
1 onion, cut in 6 wedges

12 new redskin potatoes,
  halved, or 4 to 6 large
  russet potatoes, peeled
  and quartered
2 14-1/2 oz. cans beef broth
2 bay leaves

Combine seasonings in a cup, using larger amounts for a larger roast. Moisten roast and rub seasonings into all surfaces. Place seasoned roast in a 6-quart slow cooker. Surround roast with vegetables; tuck in bay leaves. Pour broth into slow cooker. Cover and cook on low setting for 6 to 8 hours. Discard bay leaves. Serve roast on a platter, surrounded with vegetables. Serves 6 to 8.

Variations:

Italian Pot Roast & Pasta: Top seasoned roast with one can beef broth and one 26-ounce jar pasta sauce; proceed as above. Serve roast with cooked pasta; garnish with grated Parmesan cheese.

Spicy South-of-the-Border Pot Roast Burritos: Surround seasoned roast with onion wedges. Top roast with one can beef broth and one 10-ounce can diced tomatoes & green chiles, undrained; proceed as above. Shred roast and serve on tortillas, garnished with salsa, sour cream and shredded cheese.

Simply Delicious DESSERTS

Double Chocolate Brownies

Mary Alice Dobbert
King George, VA

My family's favorite brownies! I love to bake for my family, and these brownies are always a huge success. They travel well too.

1-1/2 c. all-purpose flour
1 c. baking cocoa
1/2 t. baking powder
1/2 t. salt
2/3 c. butter-flavored shortening

2 c. sugar
4 eggs
2 c. semi-sweet chocolate chips, divided

Stir together flour, cocoa, baking powder and salt in a bowl; set aside. In a large bowl, combine shortening, sugar and eggs; beat until creamy. Gradually beat in flour mixture. Stir in 1-1/2 cups chocolate chips. Pour batter into a greased 13"x9" baking pan. Bake at 350 degrees for 25 to 30 minutes, until a toothpick inserted in the center comes out clean. Sprinkle remaining chips on top; let stand 5 minutes, until chips melt; spread with a spatula to frost brownies. Cool completely in pan on a wire rack. Cut into squares. Makes 2 dozen.

For best results when baking, let eggs and butter stand at room temperature at least 30 minutes before using. Short on time? Place eggs in a bowl of warm water up to 15 minutes. Grate chilled sticks of butter with a cheese grater.

Morning Break No-Bakes

Judy Taylor
Butler, MO

I have made many less-than-successful attempts at chocolate no-bake cookies. At work on morning break, my co-workers were sharing helpful hints with me...I combined my recipe with their advice and haven't had a failure since!

1/2 c. butter	1 t. vanilla extract
2 c. sugar	3 c. quick-cooking oats,
1/2 c. milk	uncooked
3 to 4 T. baking cocoa	1/2 c. creamy peanut butter

Combine butter, sugar, milk and 3 tablespoons cocoa in a heavy saucepan, using 4 tablespoons cocoa if a deeper chocolate flavor is desired. Over medium heat, bring mixture to a full boil; continue boiling for exactly 2 minutes. Remove from heat; stir in vanilla. Add oats and stir; add peanut butter and stir. Drop by heaping teaspoonfuls onto a wax paper-lined baking sheet; let stand until set. Makes 2 dozen.

Serve hot spiced coffee with Morning Break No-Bakes.
Simply add 3/4 teaspoon apple pie spice to 1/2 cup ground coffee
and brew as usual.

Peanut Butter & Jelly Bars

Heather Tallman
Bargersville, IN

Every time I hear "peanut butter...jelly" I hear my two sons sing that cute song by the same name. Last night was no exception. I told them what I was making for dessert and they serenaded me as I cut up the strawberries. This recipe is pretty easy, I promise.

3/4 c. butter, room temperature
3/4 c. creamy peanut butter
1 c. light brown sugar, packed
1/2 c. sugar
2 t. baking powder
1/4 t. salt
2 eggs

1 t. vanilla extract
2-1/4 c. all-purpose flour
1/2 c. strawberry jam
4 c. strawberries, hulled
    and sliced
Optional: lime zest

Line a 13"x9" baking pan with aluminum foil. Lightly spray with non-stick vegetable spray; set aside. In a large bowl, beat together butter and peanut butter with an electric mixer on medium speed. Beat in sugars, baking powder and salt until combined. Add eggs and vanilla; beat until blended. Beat in as much flour as possible with mixer; mix in remaining flour with a spatula until a thick batter forms. Spread batter in pan; smooth out with spatula. Bake at 350 degrees for 25 minutes, or until lightly golden. Cool completely in pan; invert onto a serving plate. Spread jam evenly over the top. Layer strawberries on top; sprinkle with lime zest, if desired. Cut into squares. Makes one to 1-1/4 dozen.

If brown sugar has hardened in its bag, tuck a moistened paper towel into the bag and microwave it for 20 seconds. Repeat for another 10 seconds if needed. Soft and ready to use!

Lightning Bars

Pat Barbarita
Wilmington, DE

My mother, who passed away in 2010 at age 86, made these bar cookies all my life. My family still loves them. They are called Lightning Bars because they're so quick to make using ingredients always on hand. Every time I make them and share, everyone asks for the recipe. So delicious with a cup of coffee...enjoy!

1/2 c. butter, sliced
2 eggs
1 c. sugar
1 t. vanilla extract
1 t. baking powder

1/2 t. salt
1 c. all-purpose flour
3/4 c. chopped pecans, walnuts
   or almonds

Place butter in an 8"x8" baking pan; melt in a 350-degree oven and set aside. Beat eggs in a large bowl. Add sugar, vanilla, baking powder, salt and flour; mix well. Pour melted butter into batter; stir well. Pour batter into pan; sprinkle with nuts. Bake at 350 degrees for 20 to 30 minutes, until golden and a toothpick inserted in the center comes out clean. Cool completely; cut into squares. Makes one dozen.

For perfect bar cookies and brownies, line the baking pan with aluminum foil, then grease the foil. Once the cookies have baked and cooled, lift them out onto a cutting board, where they can be neatly sliced.

Old-Fashioned Buttermilk Cookies

Vickie

*The perfect recipe for cookie cutters...especially fun for children
to help decorate with your favorite buttercream frosting!*

2 c. butter, softened
2 eggs, beaten
2 c. sugar
2 T. vanilla extract
6 c. all-purpose flour
2 t. baking soda

2 t. baking powder
1 t. salt
1 c. buttermilk
Garnish: frosting, candy
   sprinkles

In a bowl, blend together butter, eggs, sugar and vanilla; set aside.
In a large bowl, mix flour, baking soda, baking powder and salt. Add
buttermilk and butter mixture to flour mixture; stir well. Roll out dough
on a lightly floured surface; cut with cookie cutters and place on
ungreased baking sheets. Dough may be chilled for a few minutes if
it becomes too soft. May also drop dough onto baking sheets by
teaspoonfuls. Bake at 375 degrees for 8 to 12 minutes, until golden;
cool on wire racks. Decorate cooled cookies as desired with frosting
and sprinkles. Makes about 3 dozen cut-out cookies or 6 dozen
drop cookies.

It's fun to decorate cookies with friends! Set out lots of cookies along with
tubes of frosting, sparkly sugar, candy sprinkles and mini candies, then
just let everyone go wild. Be sure to have extras for nibbling, plus a
pitcher of icy cold milk to serve when you sample your cookie creations.

Best-Ever Gingerbread Cookies

Carolyn Hodges
Durant, OK

A favorite holiday memory of mine! To smell these cookies baking takes me way back to my childhood, with my grandmother letting me lick the spoon and the bowl.

1-1/2 c. shortening	4 t. ground ginger
2 c. sugar	4 t. cinnamon
2 eggs	1-1/2 t. ground cloves
1/2 c. molasses	1/4 t. salt
2 t. baking soda	4-1/2 c. all-purpose flour

In a large bowl, blend shortening and sugar until creamy and smooth. Add eggs and beat well; stir in molasses, baking soda, spices and salt. Stir in flour just until well blended. Form dough into golfball-size balls. May also chill dough, then roll out on a floured surface and cut with cookie cutters. Place on ungreased baking sheets. Bake at 350 degrees for 10 to 13 minutes; cool on wire racks. Makes about 3 to 4 dozen.

Chill soft cookie dough to make it easier to work with and help it hold its shape better. Cut-outs can even be chilled right on the baking sheet before baking.

Thumbprint Butter Cookies

Shirley Condy
Plainview, NY

*This recipe is a favorite of mine! It has so many variations
that it's like a new cookie each time I make it.*

1 c. butter
3/4 c. powdered sugar
2 c. all-purpose flour

1/4 t. salt
1 t. vanilla extract
Garnish: favorite-flavor jam

In a large bowl, blend butter and sugar. Add flour, salt and vanilla;
mix well. With floured hands, roll dough into one-inch balls. Place on
baking sheets, one inch apart. Make a small indentation in each ball;
fill with a small amount of jam. Bake at 350 degrees for 10 to
12 minutes, until golden. Cool on wire racks. Makes 4 to 5 dozen.

Variations:

Spice Cookies: Dip dough balls in lightly beaten egg white and sprinkle
with cinnamon-sugar. Flatten on baking sheets. Bake as above.

Crescents: Stir in one egg along with butter and sugar. Form dough
balls into crescents. Bake as above.

Sandwich Cookies: Bake as above; cool. Sandwich cookies in pairs
with melted chocolate or frosting in between.

A muffin tin makes a handy container when you're decorating
with lots of different sprinkles and colored sugars...just fill
each cup with a different garnish.

Fruit & Oat Bars

Leslie Harvie
Simpsonville, SC

*When I was a child, my mother would whip up a batch
of these yummy bars every Saturday morning.
Strawberry was my favorite flavor!*

15-1/4 oz. pkg. yellow cake mix
2-1/2 c. quick-cooking oats,
   uncooked
3/4 c. butter, melted

12-oz. jar favorite-flavor jam
   or preserves
1 T. water

In a large bowl, combine dry cake mix and oats. Add melted butter; mix until crumbly. Add half of crumb mixture to a greased 13"x9" baking pan; press firmly to cover bottom of pan. Stir together jam or preserves and water; spoon over layer in pan. Cover with remaining crumb mixture. Pat firmly to form an even layer. Bake at 375 degrees for 20 minutes. Cool and cut into bars. Makes 1-1/2 dozen.

Breezy Peanut Butter Cookies

Darlen Corkum
Canning, Nova Scotia

*Whenever my grandchildren come down to visit we make these
simple treats together...good times!*

1 c. creamy peanut butter
1 egg, beaten

1/2 c. sugar

In a bowl, stir together peanut butter, egg and sugar. Roll into one-inch balls. Place on an ungreased baking sheet; flatten with fork. Bake at 325 degrees for 12 minutes; do not overbake. Cool on a wire rack. Makes about 2 dozen.

Parchment paper is a baker's best friend. Place it on a baking sheet to keep cookies from spreading and sticking. Clean-up is a breeze too... just toss away the paper.

Best Peanut Butter Cookies Ever

Erin Stamile
Waco, TX

Living as a hall director on a college campus, I make this cookie dough and roll it into balls to keep in my freezer. When students pop in I just turn the oven on and minutes later they are enjoying the warm, sweet aroma of homemade treats. I guarantee everyone will ask for the recipe and say, "These are the best cookies I've ever had!"

2 c. butter, softened
2 c. brown sugar, packed
3 c. sugar, divided
4 eggs, beaten
1 c. creamy peanut butter
6 c. all-purpose flour

1 T. baking soda
1 c. milk chocolate chips
1 c. chocolate chunks or
    candy-coated chocolates
1 c. peanut butter chips

In a very large bowl, using a stand mixer if possible, blend together butter, brown sugar and 2 cups sugar; add eggs and peanut butter. In a separate bowl, stir together flour and baking soda; add 1/3 at a time to butter mixture. Mix in chocolates and peanut butter chips. With an ice cream scoop, roll dough into balls by 1/4 cupfuls; roll in remaining sugar. Freeze dough balls for at least one hour; this step results in crisp edges and gooey centers. Place dough balls on ungreased baking sheets or a pizza stone, one inch apart. Bake at 350 degrees for 14 to 18 minutes, until tops just barely begin to turn golden. Cool on wire racks. Makes about 4 dozen.

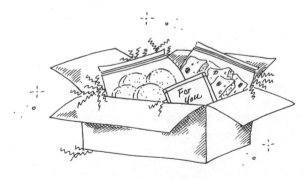

Mailing cookies to a friend? Select sturdy cookies that won't crumble easily. Bar cookies, brownies and drop cookies travel well, while frosted or filled cookies may be too soft.

Lemony Iced Oatmeal Cookies

Pat Beach
Fisherville, KY

My daughter Toni makes about 12 dozen of these delicious cookies annually for Teacher Appreciation Week at her children's elementary school. They have been requested by the staff for several years and are always a big hit.

1 c. shortening
1 c. brown sugar, packed
1 c. sugar
2 eggs
1-1/4 c. all-purpose flour
1 t. baking soda

1/2 t. salt
1/2 t. vanilla extract
3 c. long-cooking oats, uncooked
1 c. chopped pecans

In a large bowl, combine shortening, sugars and eggs. Beat thoroughly with an electric mixer on medium speed; set aside. In a separate bowl, stir together flour, baking soda and salt. Beat flour mixture into shortening mixture. Stir in vanilla and oats; fold in pecans. Drop dough by tablespoonfuls onto greased baking sheets. Bake at 350 degrees for 10 to 13 minutes, until golden. Cool on wire racks; frost with Powdered Sugar Icing. Makes 3 dozen.

Powdered Sugar Icing:

1 c. margarine, melted
1/4 c. milk
1 t. vanilla extract

1-1/2 t. lemon extract, or to taste
4 c. powdered sugar

Place margarine, milk and extracts in a large bowl. Beat in powdered sugar with an electric mixer on low, then medium speed until smooth.

My advice to you is not to inquire why or whither,
but just enjoy your ice cream while it is on your plate.
– Thornton Wilder

Chocolate-Cherry Cobbler

Arlene Smulski
Lyons, IL

Top with dollops of whipped cream...luscious!

1/4 c. butter, melted
1/2 t. vanilla extract
30-oz. can cherry pie filling
1 c. all-purpose flour

1 c. sugar
1-1/2 t. baking powder
1/4 c. baking cocoa
1/2 c. milk

In a small bowl, combine melted butter and vanilla; spread mixture in a 13"x9" baking pan. Pour pie filling into pan; set aside. In a bowl, mix together flour, sugar, baking powder and cocoa. Stir in milk. Pour batter over pie filling; do not stir. Bake at 350 degrees for 30 to 40 minutes, until golden. Serve warm. Makes 4 to 6 servings.

Cup of Cobbler

Donna Elliott
Winchester, TN

My simple fruit cobbler recipe tastes as good as my granny's!

1/2 c. butter, sliced
1 c. all-purpose flour
1 c. sugar
1 c. milk

15-oz. can sliced peaches,
cherries or blackberries
in syrup

Add butter to a lightly greased one-quart casserole dish; melt in a 350-degree oven. In a bowl, stir together flour, sugar and milk; pour batter into melted butter. Pour undrained fruit over top; do not stir. Bake at 350 degrees for 30 to 40 minutes, until bubbly and golden. Serve warm. Serves 4 to 6.

Canned fruit pie filling is different from canned fruit in syrup...be sure to double-check which kind is called for in cobbler & crisp recipes.

#8P - Equipment & Dairy Recipes

17 - Better Than Plain Hashbrowns
21 - Lemon Blueberry Coffee Cake
26 - Sausage & Pecan Casserole
30 - Dreamy orange Muffins
38 - Garlic Cheddar Beer Biscuits
47 - Cheddar Corn Muffins
51 - Sour Cream Cucumber Salad
60 - Hawaiian Salad
68 - Loaded Potato Salad
72 - Tasty Tuna in A Tomato
81 - Simple Vegetable Soup
89 - Taco Beef Soup
98 - Farmhouse Baked Mac & Cheese
101 - Hashbrown Parmesan Potatoes
103 - Broccoli "Rice" Bake
121 - Lima Beans + Bacon
137 - No-Peek Chicken & Rice
146 - Taco Hot Bake

149 - Marinated Roast
151 - Oven Barbecued Ribs
151 - Family - Favorite Pork Chops
155 - Chicken Parmesan
162 - Never-Fail Beef Stew
167 - Morning Break - No Bake
169 - Lightning Bars
172 - Thumbprint Butter Cookies
173 - Fruit & Oat Bars
173 - Energy Peanut Butter Cookies
176 - Cup of Cobbler
179 - A Farmhouse Peach Cobbler
180 - Cousin Vanilla Pudding & Variations
184 - Unincle-out Cake
189 - Dark Best Pecan Pie
189 - Delicious Pumpkin Dessert
194 - June Bug's & Tangy Marshmallow
207 - Cheesy Sausage Dips

Granny's Apple Crisp

Charlotte Smith
Tyrone, PA

My family loves, loves, loves this, and it's so easy to make.

4 c. Granny Smith apples,
   peeled, cored and sliced
1 T. lemon juice
1 c. long-cooking oats,
   uncooked
1/3 c. all-purpose flour

1/2 c. brown sugar, packed
1 t. cinnamon
1/2 t. salt
1/2 c. butter, melted
Garnish: vanilla ice cream

Arrange apple slices in a greased 9"x9" baking pan; sprinkle with lemon juice and set aside. In a bowl, mix together remaining ingredients except garnish until crumbly; sprinkle over apples. Bake at 375 degrees for 30 to 45 minutes, or until apples are tender and top is golden. Serve warm with ice cream. Makes 6 servings.

Fruit pies, crisps and cobblers can be frozen up to four months, so you can bake desserts with ripe summer fruit and serve them at Thanksgiving! Cool completely, then wrap well in plastic wrap and two layers of aluminum foil before freezing. To serve, thaw overnight in the fridge, bring to room temperature and rewarm in the oven.

Grandma's Peach Cobbler

Wendell Mays
Barboursville, WV

This is an awesome recipe, one my grandmother made very often. We could eat it daily! The almond extract and sprinkle of cinnamon were Grandma's special touches. A great comfort food that's so simple, any honeymooner could make it.

1/2 c. butter, sliced
15-1/4 oz. can sliced peaches
   in syrup
1 c. self-rising flour
1 c. sugar

1 c. milk
1 t. almond extract
cinnamon to taste
Optional: whipping cream or
   vanilla ice cream

Add butter to an 11"x7" baking pan; melt in a 350-degree oven. Pour peaches with syrup into pan; set aside. In a bowl, combine flour, sugar, milk and extract; stir until smooth. Pour batter over peaches. Bake at 350 degrees until bubbly and golden, about 35 to 45 minutes. Remove from oven; immediately sprinkle with cinnamon. Serve warm, topped with cream or ice cream, if desired. Serves 6 to 8.

Dig into Grandma's recipe box for that extra-special dessert you remember...and then bake it to share with the whole family!

Grandma Zora's Bread Pudding

Suzanne Avery
Corning, NY

This recipe was handed down from my mother's mother.
It is one of the best bread puddings I've ever tasted.

4 c. coarse bread, broken up
2 c. milk
1/4 c. butter, melted and slightly
   cooled
1/2 c. sugar

2 eggs, lightly beaten
1/2 c. raisins
1 t. cinnamon
1/4 t. salt

Place bread in a lightly greased 1-1/2 quart casserole dish; set aside. In a saucepan over medium heat, bring milk just to boiling; pour over bread. Let cool. Stir together remaining ingredients in a bowl; pour over bread mixture. Bake at 350 degrees for 45 minutes, or until a knife inserted in the center tests clean. Serve warm with Vanilla Sauce. Makes 4 to 6 servings.

Vanilla Sauce:

1 c. sugar
2 T. cornstarch
2 c. boiling water

1/4 c. butter, sliced
2 t. vanilla extract

In a saucepan over medium heat, mix together sugar and cornstarch; gradually stir in boiling water. Bring to a boil. Boil for one minute, stirring constantly. Stir in butter and vanilla.

Bread pudding is a delicious way to use up day-old bread. Try French bread, raisin bread or even leftover doughnuts and cinnamon buns for an extra-tasty dessert.

Classic Vanilla Pudding

Andrea Heyart
Aubrey, TX

This versatile pudding recipe has been a staple in my home for years.
Wonderful on its own...it also makes a delicious pie filling.

1 c. sugar
1/4 c. cornstarch
1/8 t. salt
4 egg yolks

2-1/4 c. whole milk
2 T. butter
1-1/2 t. vanilla extract

Combine sugar, cornstarch and salt in a medium saucepan. Slowly whisk in egg yolks, then milk. Cook over medium heat; whisk continuously until mixture has thickened and comes to a low boil. Continue cooking and whisking for 2 minutes. Remove from heat. Add vanilla and butter. Stir until butter has melted. Allow to cool slightly; pour into individual dessert bowls or a baked pie crust. Cover and refrigerate until chilled completely. Makes 6 to 8 servings.

Variations:

Chocolate Pudding: Reduce sugar to 3/4 cup. Add one cup semi-sweet chocolate chips along with butter; stir until melted.

Peanut Butter Pudding: Reduce sugar to 3/4 cup. Add one cup peanut butter chips along with butter; stir until melted.

Spoon individual portions of pudding into mini canning jars
for a sweet treat that can go right into lunchboxes.

Dutch Apple Creamy Cobbler

Laurel Perry
Loganville, GA

A wonderful old-fashioned dessert.

1 c. graham cracker crumbs
3 T. butter, melted
14-oz. can sweetened condensed
    milk
1/4 c. lemon juice

8-oz. container sour cream
21-oz. can apple pie filling
3/4 c. chopped walnuts
1/2 t. cinnamon
1/4 t. nutmeg

In an 8"x8" baking pan, stir together cracker crumbs and melted butter with a fork. Press mixture down with fork to form a crust; set aside. In a bowl, stir together condensed milk and lemon juice; stir in sour cream. Spread condensed milk mixture over crust. Spoon pie filling over top. Bake at 400 degrees for 15 minutes, or until hot and bubbly. Combine walnuts and spices in a small bowl; sprinkle on top. Serve warm. Makes 6 to 8 servings.

Warm caramel ice cream topping makes a delightful drizzle over
Dutch Apple Creamy Cobbler. Just heat it in the microwave for
a few seconds, and it's ready to spoon over desserts.

Rich Chocolate Cake

Gloria Robertson
Midland, TX

A luscious chocolate cake that's perfect for special occasions or sharing with friends over coffee.

2 c. all-purpose flour
1-2/3 c. sugar
5 T. baking cocoa
4 t. baking powder
1 t. salt
2/3 c. shortening

1-1/3 c. evaporated milk
1/2 c. water
3 eggs
1-1/3 t. vanilla extract
1 t. butter flavoring

In a large bowl, mix together flour, sugar, cocoa, baking powder and salt. Add remaining ingredients. Beat with an electric mixer on high speed for 2 minutes. Pour batter into a greased 13"x9" baking pan. May also use two 8"x8" baking pans or two 8" round cake pans. Bake at 350 degrees for 30 minutes. Spread Cocoa Icing over cooled cake. Makes 10 to 12 servings.

Cocoa Icing:

5 T. shortening, melted
1/3 c. baking cocoa
3 c. powdered sugar

1 T. warm milk
1-1/3 t. vanilla extract
1 t. butter flavoring

In a large bowl, stir together melted shortening and cocoa. Beat in powdered sugar, one cup at a time; add remaining ingredients. Beat until smooth.

A no-mess method for greasing and flouring baking pans: Simply grease the pan, sprinkle generously with flour, cover with plastic wrap and shake!

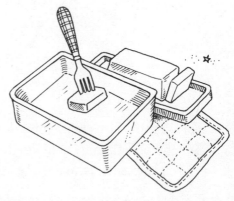

Chocolate Chip-Banana Cake

Devi McDonald
Visalia, CA

This is my mom's recipe for a deliciously moist cake. She baked it for us for every occasion, whether to make a good day even better or to cheer us on a bad day.

1/2 c. butter, softened
1 c. sugar
2 eggs, beaten
2 bananas, mashed
1 t. vanilla extract

3/4 t. baking soda
1/2 t. salt
1/2 t. cinnamon
1-1/4 c. all-purpose flour
1 c. semi-sweet chocolate chips

In a bowl, blend butter and sugar. Add eggs, bananas, vanilla, baking soda, salt and cinnamon; beat well. Stir in flour; fold in chocolate chips. Pour batter into a greased 8"x8" baking pan. Bake at 350 degrees for 35 to 40 minutes, until a toothpick inserted in the center of the cake comes out clean. Allow cake to cool in pan for 15 to 20 minutes; spoon Glaze over the top. Makes 8 servings.

Glaze:

1/4 c. butter, softened
1 t. vanilla extract

2 T. milk
2 c. powdered sugar

In a bowl, blend butter, vanilla and milk. Beat in powdered sugar until smooth.

Turn a tried & true cake recipe into yummy cupcakes! Fill greased muffin cups 2/3 full of cake batter. Bake at 350 degrees until a toothpick tests clean, about 18 to 20 minutes. Cool and frost.

Inside-Out Cake

Delania Owen
Jonesboro, AR

This recipe is fondly referred to as "the church lady cake" because when I was a young music minister's wife, a dear lady in the church shared it with me. It's quick & easy, never fails and is always a hit. I've even made it in mini Bundt® pans to give to all the teachers at school for Christmas gifts. Great served warm!

2 to 3 T. sugar
15-1/4 oz. pkg. yellow cake mix
4 eggs
1 c. oil
1 c. water
15-oz. can coconut-pecan
  frosting
1/2 c. chopped pecans

Generously spray a 10" Bundt® pan with non-stick vegetable spray. Dust pan with sugar; set aside. In a large bowl, combine dry cake mix, eggs, oil, and water; beat as directed on package. Stir in frosting and mix well; fold in nuts. Pour batter into pan. Bake at 350 degrees for 50 to 60 minutes. Let cake cool in pan for 10 minutes only; turn out onto a serving plate. Makes 12 servings.

When decorating a cake, tuck strips of wax paper under the edges of the bottom layer. Remove them after the cake is frosted for a neat and tidy cake plate with no smudges.

Charlie's Cheesecake

Geraldine Panzer
Stormville, NY

A dear friend shared this scrumptious recipe with me.

4 8-oz. pkgs. cream cheese,
   softened
6 eggs, divided
1-1/4 c. sugar

1-1/2 t. vanilla extract
1/2 c. sour cream
2/3 c. whipping cream

In a large bowl, combine cream cheese, 2 eggs, sugar and vanilla. Beat with an electric mixer on medium speed until creamy. Add remaining eggs, sour cream and whipping cream; beat well. Pour into a greased 9" or 10" springform pan. Bake on center rack of oven at 350 degrees for 45 minutes. Turn oven to broil; broil for 3 to 4 minutes, until golden. Reset oven to 350 degrees; turn off oven. Allow cheesecake to cool in oven for 45 minutes. Remove to a wire rack; cool completely, then chill. Serves 10 to 12.

Buttery Pound Cake

Sue Franks
Lexington, NC

In the 20 years I've been using this recipe, it has never failed me.

1/2 c. butter, softened
1 c. sugar
3 eggs
8-oz. container sour cream
1 c. self-rising flour

16-1/2 oz. golden butter
   cake mix
2/3 c. milk
1 t. lemon extract

In a large bowl, beat butter and sugar with an electric mixer on medium speed. Add eggs, one at a time, beating well after each addition. Stir in sour cream. Beat in flour and dry cake mix alternately with milk; beat well. Stir in extract. Pour batter into a greased and floured Bundt® pan. Bake at 325 degrees for about one hour, or until a toothpick inserted in the center tests clean. Cool slightly; turn cake out onto a serving plate. Serves 12 to 16.

Great-Gramma Starr's Spice Cake

Janis Parr
Campbellford, Ontario

My Gramma Starr baked well into her 80s. We kids loved to visit her and never knew what delicious treat would await us...this cake was a favorite. There was a huge old tree in her backyard that we would climb with a basket of Gramma's spice cake, and there we would sit and enjoy it to the very last crumb.

1-1/2 c. all-purpose flour	1/4 t. ground ginger
1 c. sugar	1/4 t. ground cloves
1 T. baking powder	1/3 c. shortening
1 t. salt	2/3 c. milk, divided
1/4 t. cream of tartar	2 eggs
1/2 t. cinnamon	1-1/4 t. vanilla extract
1/2 t. nutmeg	Garnish: favorite frosting

In a large bowl, stir together flour, sugar, baking powder, salt, cream of tartar and spices. Add shortening and 1/3 cup milk. Beat with an electric mixer on medium speed for 2 minutes. Add eggs, remaining milk and vanilla; beat for one additional minute. Pour batter into a greased 8"x8" baking pan. Bake at 350 degrees for 40 to 45 minutes, until a toothpick inserted in the center tests clean. Cool; frost as desired. Makes 6 to 8 servings.

Cakes are usually done when the sides start to pull away from the pan. Test for doneness by inserting a wooden toothpick in or near the center...it should come out clean, with no batter on it.

Never-Fail Gingerbread Cake

Vicky Brown
Beaver Dam, KY

My grandmother always baked this spicy cake on cold damp winter evenings. A delicious aroma of gingerbread would welcome my family as we came home for supper. Now I make this to share with friends and to celebrate the holidays.

1 c. butter, melted
1 c. sugar
1 c. molasses
4 c. all-purpose flour
2 t. baking soda
1 t. salt

2 t. ground ginger
2 t. cinnamon
2 c. hot water
Garnish: butter or whipped
   cream and cinnamon

In a large bowl, stir together butter, sugar and molasses; set aside. Combine flour, baking soda, salt and spices in a separate bowl; mix well. Add flour mixture to butter mixture alternately with hot water; beat until smooth. Pour batter into a greased 13"x9" baking pan. Bake at 350 degrees for 45 minutes, or until a toothpick inserted in the center tests clean. Serve squares of cake warm with a pat of butter on top. May also let cool and top with a dollop of whipped cream and a sprinkle of cinnamon. Makes 16 servings.

Make sure you're baking with fresh spices...take a sniff test!
Hold the open container at chin level. If you can't detect the aroma
of the spice, it's time for a new jar.

Chocolate Meringue Pie

Jessica Adams
Galax, VA

This recipe is simple and quick and it is sure to please! It was the first recipe I ever learned to follow. It's my constant go-to for family reunions and gatherings...I always take home an empty pie plate. Enjoy!

9-inch deep-dish pie crust
3 eggs, separated
1 c. sugar
6 T. butter, melted and slightly cooled

5-oz. can evaporated milk
3 T. all-purpose flour
3 T. baking cocoa
1 t. vanilla extract

Arrange pie crust in a 9" deep-dish pie plate; set aside. Combine egg yolks and remaining ingredients in a bowl. Mix well and pour into unbaked pie crust. Bake at 350 degrees for 45 to 50 minutes, until pie is firm when jiggled. Gently spread Meringue over pie filling, making sure that it touches the pie crust all the way around. Bake at 350 degrees for an additional 5 to 10 minutes, until meringue is golden. Cool completely before slicing. Makes 8 servings.

Meringue:

3 egg whites, reserved
    from filling

2 T. sugar
1/2 t. vanilla extract

In a deep bowl, beat egg whites with an electric mixer on high speed for about 5 minutes, until soft peaks form. Beat in sugar and vanilla.

To separate eggs when there's no egg separator handy, crack each egg into a cup and pour it through a slotted spoon. The egg white will run through the slots, leaving the yolk behind on the spoon.

Dad's Best Pecan Pie

Debra Caraballo
Manahawkin, NJ

When my dad found this recipe in a magazine years ago, it became his job to make these pecan pies for the holidays! I treasure so much the memory of him in the kitchen putting them together.

1/3 c. butter
1 c. sugar
1 c. light corn syrup
4 eggs, beaten

1/4 t. salt
1 t. vanilla extract
1 c. chopped pecans
9-inch pie crust

Combine butter, sugar, and corn syrup in a medium saucepan. Cook over low heat, stirring constantly, under butter melts and sugar dissolves. Remove from heat; let cool for about 10 minutes. Add beaten eggs, salt and vanilla; stir well. Pour into unbaked pie crust; arrange pecans on top. Bake at 325 degrees for 50 minutes. Cool completely before cutting. Makes 8 servings.

Delicious Pumpkin Dessert

Sandra Monroe
Preston, MD

This recipe was found in a church cookbook that is almost 50 years old. I make it often for my family...everybody loves it!

18-1/4 oz. pkg. yellow cake
   mix, divided
1/2 c. plus 3 T. butter, divided
4 eggs, divided
29-oz. can pumpkin

1/2 c. brown sugar, packed
2/3 c. milk
1 t. cinnamon
1/2 c. sugar
1/2 c. chopped pecans

Set aside one cup dry cake mix for topping. In a bowl, combine remaining cake mix, 1/2 cup melted butter and one egg; beat well. Spread batter in a 13"x9" baking pan sprayed with non-stick vegetable spray; set aside. In a separate bowl, stir together pumpkin, remaining eggs, brown sugar, milk and cinnamon; spread over batter. Combine reserved cake mix with sugar. Cut in remaining butter until crumbly; sprinkle over pumpkin mixture. Top with pecans. Bake at 350 degrees for 40 to 45 minutes, testing for doneness with a toothpick. Serves 10.

Mom's Apple Pie

Kelly Rincan
Manchester, NH

Mom used to make this pie for my family ever since I was a little girl. It reminds me of my family being together, all seven of us. I have now started the tradition with my own family...they love it! With a batter topping and no bottom crust, it's a snap to make.

5 to 6 Cortland or Granny Smith
    apples, peeled, cored
    and sliced
1 t. cinnamon
1 c. plus 1 T. sugar, divided
1 c. all-purpose flour
3/4 c. butter, melted and
    slightly cooled
1 egg, beaten
1/8 t. salt
Optional: 1/2 c. chopped walnuts

Arrange apple slices in a greased 9" or 10" pie plate, filling 3/4 full. Sprinkle with cinnamon and one tablespoon sugar; set aside. In a bowl, mix together remaining sugar and other ingredients; pour over apples. Bake at 350 degrees for 50 minutes, or until golden and apples are tender. Makes 6 to 8 servings.

Set a filled pie plate on a baking sheet before popping it in the oven. The baking sheet will catch any juices that may drip and allow the pie's bottom crust to bake more evenly.

APPETIZERS
for
Sharing

Garlic Cheese Ball

Lynne McKaige
Apple Valley, MN

*Whenever I bring this cheese ball to a party, people flock to it.
So creamy and delicious, you can't resist!*

8-oz. pkg. cream cheese,
    softened
2 5-oz. jars sharp pasteurized
    process cheese sauce
1/2 c. butter, softened

1 to 2 cloves garlic, pressed
5 drops hot pepper sauce
paprika, salt and pepper to taste
1 c. finely chopped pecans
crackers

In a large bowl, combine all ingredients except pecans and crackers.
Blend well; cover and refrigerate until very firm. Just before serving
time, spread pecans on a length of wax paper. Turn out cheese mixture
and form into a ball; roll in pecans until coated. Serve cheese ball with
crackers. Serves 8 to 10.

Keep party time super-simple. Serve one or two tried & true
appetizers like cheese balls and dips, and pick up some tasty
go-withs like pickles, marinated olives and cocktail nuts
at the grocery store. Relax and enjoy your guests!

Easy Ranch Cheese Ball

Carolyn Tyler
Hamilton, AL

I came up with this recipe one day when I needed an appetizer to take to a get-together. It was a hit! It's really simple to make... great for new cooks.

2 8-oz. pkgs. cream cheese, softened
1-oz. pkg. ranch salad dressing mix
Optional: 1 bunch green onions, chopped

3/4 c. bacon bits or chopped pecans
assorted crackers or cut-up vegetables

In a large bowl, combine cream cheese, dip mix and onions, if using. Blend thoroughly and form into a ball. Wrap in plastic wrap; refrigerate at least 2 hours, until firm. Just before serving time, roll cheese ball in bacon bits or pecans on a length of wax paper. Serve cheese ball with crackers or vegetables. Makes 15 to 25 servings.

Cheesy Artichoke Dip

Sue Rasmussen
New Richmond, WI

This is the best artichoke dip I have ever tasted. It is delicious and so fast to put together! I sampled it at a friend's party and begged for the recipe. Now it is a favorite at all our gatherings.

16-oz. pkg. shredded Parmesan cheese
8-oz. pkg. shredded mozzarella cheese
1 c. mayonnaise

2 c. canned artichoke hearts, drained and chopped
1 T. garlic, minced
pita chips or sliced French bread

In a large bowl, mix together all ingredients except pita chips and bread. Spread in a greased 13"x9" baking pan. Bake, uncovered, at 350 degrees for 20 to 30 minutes, until bubbly and edges are lightly golden. Serve with pita chips or French bread. Makes 12 to 15 servings.

193

Jim's Sweet & Tangy Meatballs

Jim Bohner
Harrisburg, PA

These tasty meatballs are sure to please a crowd. It takes just two minutes to put them together, then I'm set for a party!

32-oz. pkg. frozen meatballs
2 12-oz. bottles chili sauce
1 c. catsup

1/4 c. mustard
3 T. brown sugar, packed

Mix all ingredients together in a slow cooker. Cover and cook on low setting for 2 to 4 hours, until hot and meatballs are cooked through. Makes 10 servings.

Take a stroll through your neighborhood dollar store where all kinds of colorful, clever items for table decorating, serving and party favors can be found...big fun at a small price!

Bacon-Brown Sugar Sausages

Taylor Morris
Oregon City, OR

My fiance and I love these sausages...they're perfect for football parties. Sometimes I'll use maple or pepper bacon to add even more flavor.

1 lb. bacon, cut into thirds
14-oz. pkg. mini smoked
   sausages

1/2 c. butter, melted
1-3/4 c. brown sugar, packed
   and divided

In a skillet over medium heat, cook bacon until partially cooked but not crisp; drain. Wrap each sausage in a piece of bacon; place in a single layer in an ungreased 13"x9" baking pan. In a bowl, mix melted butter and one cup brown sugar; spoon over sausages. Sprinkle remaining brown sugar evenly over sausages. Bake, uncovered, at 375 degrees for 15 to 25 minutes. Increase oven temperature to 400 degrees. Bake an additional 5 minutes, or until bacon is crisp and brown sugar is all dissolved. Serves 6 to 8.

Poppin' Pork Bites

Connie Hilty
Pearland, TX

A most-requested recipe...great for game day!

1 lb. pork tenderloin, cut
   crosswise, 1/2-inch thick
2 eggs, beaten
1 c. buttermilk
1 c. all-purpose flour
1 t. garlic powder

1 t. onion powder
1 t. pepper
oil for frying
Garnish: honey mustard,
   barbecue sauce

Pound pork slices to 1/4-inch thickness; cut each slice into 4 pieces. Whisk together eggs and buttermilk in a shallow dish. Mix flour and seasonings in another dish. Dip each piece into egg mixture, then flour mixture. Heat oil in a large skillet over medium heat. Working in batches, cook 4 to 5 minutes per side, or until golden and juices run clear. Serve with sauces for dipping. Serves 4 to 6.

Fresh Veggie Pizza

Amy Jordan
Lily, KY

*An oldie but goodie! We love it for family fun night at home.
Add any other crunchy fresh vegetables you like.*

8-oz. tube refrigerated reduced-
fat crescent rolls
8-oz. pkg. reduced-fat cream
cheese
1-oz. pkg. ranch salad dressing
mix
2 T. fat-free milk

1/2 c. broccoli, chopped
1/2 c. cauliflower, chopped
1/2 c. carrots, peeled and
chopped
1/2 c. green pepper, chopped
1/2 c. mushrooms, chopped

Spray a 13"x9" baking pan with non-stick vegetable spray. Unroll
crescent rolls but do not separate; press rolls into bottom of pan. Bake
at 375 degrees for 11 to 13 minutes, until golden. Cool completely. In
a bowl, beat together cream cheese, dressing mix and milk until
smooth. Spread mixture over baked crust; sprinkle with vegetables.
Cover and refrigerate for one hour before serving; cut into squares.
Serves 6 to 8.

Swap party specialties with a friend! For example, offer to trade
a kettle of your super-secret-recipe chili for a dozen or two of
your best girlfriend's fabulous cupcakes. It's a super way
to save party-planning time and money.

Tuscan Valley Dip

Annette Ceravolo
Hoover, AL

Perfected over the years, this dip is so creamy and filled with savory flavor. It's always popular at parties...guests will definitely be asking you for the recipe.

2 8-oz. pkgs. cream cheese, softened
2 T. sour cream
3/4 c. sun-dried tomatoes (not oil-packed), finely chopped
1 c. sliced black olives, drained
1/4 c. red onion, finely chopped
assorted crackers and cut-up vegetables

In a bowl, stir together cream cheese and sour cream until well blended. Add tomatoes, olives and onion; mix well. Cover and refrigerate 8 hours to overnight so flavors can blend. Let stand at room temperature for 30 minutes before serving. Serve with crackers and vegetables. Makes 4 cups.

Serve easy-to-handle foods and beverages at tables in several different rooms around the house. Guests will be able to snack and mingle easily.

Pepperoni Squares

Lori Ritchey
Denver, PA

Company coming and you need a quick appetizer? This will give your guests a warm welcome!

2 c. milk
2 eggs, beaten
1-1/2 c. all-purpose flour
1 lb. Muenster cheese, diced
8-oz. pkg. pepperoni, chopped

1/2 t. dried oregano
1/4 t. dried parsley
1/4 t. pepper
1 c. shredded pizza-blend cheese
Garnish: warmed pizza sauce

Combine milk, eggs, flour, Muenster cheese, pepperoni and spices in a large bowl. Mix well; pour into a lightly greased 13"x9" baking pan. Bake at 350 degrees for 25 minutes. Remove from oven; sprinkle with pizza-blend cheese. Bake for an additional 5 to 8 minutes, until melted. Cool slightly; cut into squares. Serve with pizza sauce for dipping. Serves 8 to 10.

An instant appetizer that's always a hit! Unwrap a block of cream cheese and place it on a serving plate. Top with spicy pepper sauce or fruity chutney. Serve with crisp crackers and a cheese spreader.

Kacie's Pizza Balls

Kacie Johnston
Danville, NH

Having four babies with springtime birthdays, I found this recipe is a crowd-pleaser for all ages at my little ones' parties! It is really versatile too. I have swapped in different cheeses, sauces and have tried both fresh and dried herbs...it's always delicious.

2 7-1/2 oz. tubes refrigerated
    biscuits
20 slices pepperoni
2 c. shredded pizza-blend cheese

1 T. Italian seasoning or
    dried basil
2 T. grated Parmesan cheese
1 c. pizza sauce

Spray a 13"x9" glass baking pan with non-stick vegetable spray; set aside. Separate biscuits; flatten with the palm of your hand. Top each biscuit with a pepperoni slice and some pizza-blend cheese. Fold over edges of biscuit, forming a ball; pinch together. Place balls in pan, seam-side down, about 1/4-inch apart. Sprinkle with seasoning and Parmesan cheese. Bake at 450 degrees for 8 to 10 minutes, just until tops and edges start to turn golden. Cool for a few minutes; remove rolls from pan and pull apart. Place rolls on a serving plate, with dipping sauce on the side. Serves 10.

A good rule of thumb for appetizers...serve six to eight pieces per person if dinner will follow. Plan for 12 to 15 per person if it's an appetizer-only gathering.

Anne's Amazing Chicken Wings

Lisa Zamfino
Fairfield, CT

This recipe won a contest in our local paper for best wings.
Once you try them, you'll see why. Thanks, Anne!

1 c. soy sauce
2 c. water
1-1/4 c. dark brown sugar,
  packed

2-1/2 t. garlic powder
1-1/4 t. ground ginger
4-1/2 lbs. chicken wings

Combine all ingredients except wings in a very large bowl. Add wings; toss to coat. Cover and refrigerate 8 hours to overnight. Drain wings, discarding marinade. Place wings in a single layer on an ungreased 15"x10" jelly-roll pan. Bake at 400 degrees for 45 to 55 minutes, turning once, until golden and juices run clear when pierced. Serves 12.

Alongside sticky finger foods like chicken wings, set out a basket of washcloths, moistened with lemon-scented water and warmed briefly in the microwave. Guests will thank you!

Honey & Salsa Chicken Wings

Brenda Hager
Nancy, KY

These wings are really tasty! They make a great quick evening meal or party snack. My husband prefers boneless, skinless thighs, so I cut them in half and prepare them this way. Be sure to line the baking sheet with aluminum foil to make clean-up a snap.

1 c. favorite salsa
1/4 c. honey

1/2 t. ground ginger
1-1/2 lbs. chicken wings

In a large bowl, combine salsa, honey and ginger. Add wings; toss to coat. Place wings on an aluminum foil-lined 15"x10" jelly-roll pan. Bake at 400 degrees for 45 to 55 minutes, or until chicken juices run clear, turning once and basting with pan juices. Serves 4.

When measuring sticky ingredients like honey or molasses, spray the measuring cup with non-stick vegetable spray first. The contents will slip right out.

Party Platter Pinwheels

Nancy Johnson
Laverne, OK

*I was looking for something for our church's annual tailgating
party when I discovered this recipe. Jazz up your party platter
by using three different colors of tortilla.*

1/2 c. light mayonnaise
3-oz. pkg. reduced-fat cream
  cheese, softened
2 T. chunky salsa
1 t. Dijon mustard
6 slices bacon, crisply cooked
  and crumbled

3 8 to 10-inch spinach, tomato
  and/or plain flour tortillas
3 roma tomatoes, chopped
1-1/2 c. romaine lettuce,
  shredded

In a small bowl, blend mayonnaise, cream cheese, salsa and mustard;
stir in bacon. Spread mixture evenly over tortillas. Top with tomatoes
and lettuce. Tightly roll up tortillas; wrap individually in plastic wrap.
Refrigerate at least one hour but no longer than 8 hours. Cut into
one-inch slices; secure each slice with a toothpick. Serves 12 to 15.

For an easy yet elegant appetizer, try a cheese platter. Choose a soft
cheese, a hard cheese and a semi-soft or crumbly cheese. Add a basket
of crisp crackers, crusty baguette slices and some sliced apples
or pears. So simple, yet sure to please guests!

Irresistible Herbed Cheese

Karen Morin
Southbridge, MA

*The first time I made this dip, nobody wanted to try it. But later
I happened to look over and saw my friend pigging out on it!
This dip is also delicious spread on roast beef sandwiches.*

2 8-oz. pkgs. cream cheese,
  softened
1/2 c. butter, softened
1-oz. pkg. ranch salad
  dressing mix
2 T. Dijon mustard

1 T. garlic, minced
Optional: 1 round loaf marble
  rye bread, hollowed out
cubed French or Italian bread,
  cut-up vegetables

Combine cream cheese, butter, dressing mix, mustard and garlic in a
large bowl. Mix until creamy and well blended. Cover and refrigerate
for 8 hours to overnight. Let stand at room temperature for 30 minutes
before serving. To serve, spoon dip into hollowed-out bread loaf or a
serving dish. Serve with cut-up pieces of French or Italian bread.
Serves 12.

Susie's Pickles

Sue Lund
Indianapolis, IN

*My aunt taught me how to make these pickle slices, and I've been
requested to make them on every occasion. Everyone loves them!*

2 8-oz. pkgs. cream cheese,
  softened
32-oz. jar whole kosher dill
  pickles, drained and
  patted dry

4 2-oz. pkgs. thinly sliced deli
  beef, finely chopped

Spread each pickle all over with cream cheese; roll in chopped beef to
coat. Place pickles on a plate; cover and chill until serving time. Slice
pickles and arrange on a serving plate. Makes 25 servings.

4-Way Potato Skins

Kelly Serdynski Gray
Weston, WV

These potato skins are my number-one requested snack...I get raves about them! My family of all boys loves football night, and these are a favorite. For parties, I like to make a variety of flavors.

6 baking potatoes
8-oz. pkg. cream cheese, cut
    into 12 cubes
5 T. light olive oil
1 bunch broccoli, cut into
    flowerets

2 t. garlic salt
1 t. pepper
16-oz. pkg. shredded Cheddar
    cheese

Microwave potatoes for 10 to 11 minutes, until fork-tender. Cut potatoes in half and scoop out pulp, creating shells. Reserve potato pulp for use in another recipe. Place a cream cheese cube in each potato shell; set aside. Meanwhile, heat olive oil in a skillet over medium heat; add broccoli, garlic salt and pepper. Sauté at least 10 minutes, until broccoli is crisp-tender. Fill shells with broccoli mixture; cover completely with Cheddar cheese. Place shells in an ungreased 13"x9" baking pan. Bake, uncovered, at 350 degrees for 10 minutes, or until cheese is melted. Cool slightly before serving. Serves 4 to 6.

Variations:

Artichoke-Mozzarella Potato Skins: Prepare potatoes; add cream cheese as directed above. Replace broccoli with drained artichoke hearts; replace Cheddar cheese with mozzarella. Bake for 10 minutes.

California Potato Skins: Prepare potatoes; add cream cheese as directed above. Replace broccoli with diced cooked chicken and sliced avocado; replace Cheddar cheese with mozzarella. Bake for 10 minutes; add a dollop of sour cream.

Rodeo Potato Skins: Prepare potatoes; omit cream cheese. Replace broccoli with barbecue pulled pork, sautéed onion, garlic salt and cayenne pepper, if desired. Top with Cheddar cheese. Bake for 15 to 20 minutes, until pork is heated through.

Ranch-Stuffed Mushrooms

Mandy Mears
Lexington, SC

This is my tried & true recipe whenever I need an appetizer for a gathering. Sometimes people are standing by to gobble them up as they come out of the oven!

8-oz. pkg. cream cheese, softened
1/4 c. grated Parmesan cheese
1/4 c. mayonnaise
1-1/2 T. ranch salad dressing mix
1 T. onion, minced

2 t. dried parsley
6-oz. pkg. chicken-flavored stuffing mix
1-1/2 lbs. whole mushrooms, stems removed and discarded
1/2 c. butter, melted

In a large bowl, mix together cheeses, mayonnaise, dressing mix, onion and parsley until well blended. Spread stuffing out on a plate. Fill mushroom caps with cream cheese mixture, then press the tops into the stuffing so that a generous amount of stuffing crumbs sticks to cream cheese mixture. Place mushrooms on an aluminum foil-lined baking sheet. Drizzle melted butter over mushrooms. Bake at 375 degrees for about 30 minutes, until hot and bubbly. Cool slightly before serving. Makes 2 dozen.

A day or two before your party, set out all the serving platters, baskets and dishes and label them..."Chips & Dip," "Chicken Wings" and so on. When party time arrives, you'll be able to set out all the goodies in seconds flat.

Warm Blue Cheese Dip

Eugenia Taylor
Stroudsburg, PA

*My mom and dad had a cocktail party every year for my dad's office.
I got to be the waitress & cook for these parties. This recipe was a
favorite of mine...so easy to make and serve!*

8 slices bacon
3 to 4 cloves garlic, minced
8-oz. pkg. cream cheese,
  softened
1/4 c. half-and-half

4-oz. container crumbled
  blue cheese
2 T. fresh chives, chopped
crackers, toast slices or chips

In a skillet over medium heat, cook bacon until crisp. Remove bacon
to a paper towel; pat dry and crumble. Add garlic to drippings in skillet;
cook for about 3 minutes and remove from skillet. Combine cream
cheese and half-and-half in a bowl. Beat until smooth; stir in bacon,
garlic, blue cheese and chives. Spread in an ungreased 2-quart
casserole dish. Cover and bake at 350 degrees for 30 minutes, or until
bubbly and lightly golden. Serve warm with crackers, toast slices or
chips. Serves 6.

Boneless Buffalo Chicken Dip

Kimberly Ascroft
Merritt Island, FL

This is our go-to tailgating party dip!

2 8-oz. pkgs. cream cheese,
  softened
1 c. buffalo wing sauce,
  or to taste
1 c. ranch salad dressing

2 lbs. boneless, skinless chicken,
  cooked and cubed
2 c. shredded Mexican-blend
  cheese

In a 2-quart casserole dish, blend cream cheese, sauce and salad
dressing. Fold in chicken and cheese. Bake, uncovered, at 350 degrees
for 30 minutes, or until hot and bubbly. Serves 12 to 15.

Cheesy Sausage Dip

JoAlice Welton
Lawrenceville, GA

A tried & true party appetizer...whenever I serve it, I know there will be none left over!

1 lb. mild ground pork sausage
2 lbs. pasteurized process
   cheese, diced
10-oz. can diced tomatoes with
   green chiles

10-oz. can hot diced tomatoes
   with green chiles
nacho tortilla chips

Brown sausage in a large skillet over medium heat; drain. Reduce heat to medium-low. Add cheese and undrained tomatoes. Cook and stir until bubbly and cheese is melted. Serve warm with tortilla chips. May be served from a slow cooker set on low setting. Serves 6 to 8.

Hot & Spicy Ranch Pretzels

Monica Tull
Jennings, OK

I make this for every school event, bake sale and party, even for my husband's lunch. Everyone asks for the recipe. We like it spicy so we add even more cayenne pepper...this amount just gives it a slight kick. Try it with lemon pepper instead of cayenne too!

16-oz. pkg. pretzel twists
1 c. oil
3 T. cayenne pepper, or to taste

1-oz. pkg. ranch salad
   dressing mix

Pour pretzels into a gallon-size plastic zipping bag. In a bowl, stir together remaining ingredients. Pour over pretzels; seal bag and shake well. Lay bag flat and let stand for one hour, turning bag over every 15 minutes. Drain on paper towels; store in an airtight container. Makes one pound.

Serving up snack mix or popcorn for a crowd? Use coffee filters as disposable bowls. Afterwards, just toss 'em away!

Bacon-Wrapped Water Chestnuts

Shirley McGlin
Black Creek, WI

*My family loves these tasty tidbits! I make them up ahead of time,
then keep them warm in a slow cooker until serving time.*

2 8-oz. cans whole water
   chestnuts, drained
1 lb. bacon, cut into halves or
   thirds

1 c. catsup
1 c. sugar
2 T. soy sauce

Wrap each water chestnut in a piece of bacon; secure with a toothpick.
Place on a lightly greased broiler pan. Bake, uncovered at 350 degrees
for one hour, or until bacon is crisp. Combine remaining ingredients in
a saucepan. Cook and stir over medium-low heat until sugar dissolves.
Just before serving time, spoon catsup mixture over water chestnuts.
Serve warm. Serves 10.

Put out the welcome mat and invite friends over for a retro-style
appetizer party. Serve up yummy finger foods like Bacon-Wrapped
Water Chestnuts and play favorite tunes from the 1950s or 1960s...
everyone is sure to have a blast!

Bacon-Parmesan Dip

Renee Walston
Peoria, AZ

My hubby John loves to create in the kitchen...he is an artist when it comes to mixing ingredients! This is just one of his many recipes. It's delicious with chips, crackers and veggies.

4 slices bacon	1 t. coarse pepper
2/3 c. grated Parmesan cheese	8-oz. container sour cream
1/4 onion, sliced	2 T. mayonnaise
1 clove garlic	

In a skillet over medium heat, cook bacon until crisp; drain and crumble. Combine bacon, cheese, onion, garlic and pepper in a food processor. Pulse until all ingredients are finely chopped; transfer to a bowl. Add sour cream and mayonnaise; stir until well combined. Cover and chill for at least an hour. Makes about 2 cups.

Imperial Bacon

Dale-Harriet Rogovich
Madison, WI

So irresistible, you may want to make a double batch!

1 lb. thick-cut peppered bacon	2 T. mustard
1/3 c. brown sugar, packed	

Line a baking sheet with heavy-duty aluminum foil; set a wire rack in pan. Cut bacon slices in half, if desired. Arrange bacon in a single layer on rack. Stir together brown sugar and mustard in a cup; brush over bacon slices. Place baking sheet on top shelf of oven. Bake at 400 degrees for 15 minutes, or until partially cooked. Turn slices over with tongs; brush with glaze. Return to oven; continue baking to desired crispness. Drain bacon on paper towels. Serves 4 to 6.

A relish tray of crunchy bite-size vegetables like baby carrots, cherry tomatoes, broccoli flowerets and celery stalks is always welcome.

Doreen's Crab Dip

Denine Anderson-Regan
Bay Shore, NY

This satisfying dip has been in our family for years. My mother passed the recipe on to my sister Daniele and me. Incredibly simple to make, it's the perfect appetizer for family meals.

3/4 c. cream cheese, softened
3/4 c. mayonnaise
6-oz. can crabmeat, drained,
   rinsed and flaked
4 T. shredded Cheddar cheese,
   divided

2 T. onion, finely minced
1/2 t. lemon juice
3/4 t. Worcestershire sauce
1/8 t. salt
1/8 t. pepper
crackers

Combine cream cheese and mayonnaise in a bowl. Beat with an electric mixer on medium speed until smooth. Stir in crabmeat, 3 tablespoons Cheddar cheese, onion, lemon juice, Worcestershire sauce, salt and pepper. Spread in an ungreased 2-quart casserole dish. Bake, uncovered, at 350 degrees for 15 to 20 minutes, until hot and bubbly. Remove from oven; top with remaining cheese. Broil for one to 2 minutes, until cheese is melted. Serve warm with crackers. Makes 8 servings.

Large scallop shells make delightful serving containers for seafood dishes. Use shells you've found on a beach vacation or check party supply stores for dinner-ready shells.

Shrimp Darcy

Kristina Hill
Apopka, FL

This is a great appetizer to hold guests over until dinner is ready.
Frozen shrimp may be used...just thaw and rinse well.

3 lbs. uncooked jumbo shrimp,
    peeled and cleaned
16-oz. bottle zesty Italian salad
    dressing

2 T. garlic, pressed
2 lemons, halved
1/4 c. fresh parsley, chopped
1 loaf garlic bread, sliced

In a 13"x9" glass baking pan, combine shrimp, salad dressing and garlic. Squeeze lemons over shrimp and add lemon halves to pan, cut-side up. Sprinkle parsley on top. Bake, uncovered, at 350 degrees for 15 minutes. Stir; bake an additional 15 minutes. Serve shrimp with bread for dipping in pan juices. Makes 6 to 10 servings.

Shrimply Divine

Kathy Van Daalen
Virginia Beach, VA

A super-simple appetizer that's been in my family
for years. It's perfect for any occasion, from football parties
to elegant dinner parties.

2 8-oz. pkgs. cream cheese,
    softened
12-oz. bottle cocktail sauce,
    chilled

1 lb. cooked medium shrimp
snack crackers

Beat cream cheese in a bowl until smooth; spread on a large serving platter. Pour cocktail sauce over cream cheese; arrange shrimp on top. Serve with crackers. Makes 20 servings.

Mini Fruit Tarts with Brie

Kristin Turner
Raleigh, NC

These sweet little treats are fun to whip up for a party! Strawberry, raspberry, peach and apricot preserves as well as orange marmalade all work well, so use your favorites. I like to mix & match and offer a variety of flavors.

2 2.1-oz. pkgs. frozen mini
   phyllo cups
1/4 lb. Brie cheese, cut into
   1/2-inch cubes

1 c. white chocolate chips
3/4 c. favorite-flavor fruit
   preserves

Assemble frozen phyllo cups on a non-stick baking sheet. Fill each cup with 2 to 3 white chocolate chips, one cheese cube and one teaspoon preserves. Bake at 350 degrees for about 9 minutes, until warmed through. Serve warm or at room temperature, garnished with several more chocolate chips, if desired. Makes 2-1/2 dozen.

Don't limit your table coverings to tablecloths. Pick up a few yards of fabric that coordinates with your party theme at the craft store. No hemming required...trim the edges with pinking shears, or just tuck them under!

Nutty Cinnamon Snack Mix

Becky Bruner
Virginia Beach, VA

*I often give this snack mix as a gift...it looks yummy in a pretty jar
or gift bag. Feel free to substitute an equal amount of your
favorite nuts instead of pecans or almonds.*

3 c. apple-cinnamon doughnut-
    shaped oat cereal
2 c. pecan halves
1 c. whole almonds
1 c. chow mein noodles

2 egg whites
1 c. sugar
2 T. cinnamon
1/2 t. salt

In a large bowl, mix cereal, nuts and chow mein noodles. Spread on a
greased baking sheet. Combine remaining ingredients in a bowl; pour
over cereal mixture and stir well. Bake, uncovered, at 300 degrees for
35 to 40 minutes, stirring frequently. Cool completely; store in an
airtight container. Makes about 8 cups.

Pizza popcorn...a crunchy snack that's ready in a jiffy! Combine 1/4 cup
grated Parmesan cheese, 2 teaspoons each Italian seasoning and paprika,
and one teaspoon each onion powder and garlic powder. Sprinkle over
8 cups buttered popcorn, add salt to taste and toss to mix well.

Chocolate Chip Cheese Ball

Tracee Cummins
Amarillo, TX

I found this unusual recipe in a magazine years ago. It's a scrumptious snack that's elegant enough for a dessert buffet or to serve at a shower. I use whatever baking chips I have on hand...milk chocolate, white chocolate, peanut butter, almond brickle or a combination. It's always delicious!

8-oz. pkg. cream cheese,
   softened
1/2 c. butter, softened
1/4 t. vanilla extract
3/4 c. powdered sugar

2 T. brown sugar, packed
3/4 c. mini semi-sweet
   chocolate chips
3/4 c. finely chopped pecans
graham cracker squares or sticks

In a bowl, beat cream cheese, butter and vanilla with an electric mixer on medium speed until light and fluffy. Gradually add sugars; beat just until combined. Stir in chocolate chips. Cover and refrigerate for 2 hours. Form mixture into a ball; wrap in plastic wrap and refrigerate at least one hour. Just before serving, roll ball in pecans. Serve with graham cracker sticks or squares. Serves 10 to 12.

The golden glow of candlelight adds a magic touch to any gathering. Fill the base of a large hurricane lamp with colored glass gems or pretty beach pebbles, then top with a fat pillar candle for a delightful centerpiece.

Apples & Toffee Dip

Marla Carter
Owensboro, KY

This sweet dip is always a hit! A friend brought it to my family at the funeral home when my precious grandmother passed away. Whenever I make it, I still remember the thoughtfulness of that friend.

8-oz. pkg. cream cheese,
   softened
3/4 c. brown sugar, packed
1/2 c. powdered sugar
1 t. vanilla extract
3/4 c. toffee baking bits

6 Red Delicious apples, cored
   and cut into 8 wedges
6 Granny Smith apples, cored
   and cut into 8 wedges
1 c. pineapple juice

Combine cream cheese, sugars and vanilla in a bowl. Beat with an electric mixer on medium speed until smooth. Stir in toffee bits; cover and chill. Place apple wedges in a bowl or large plastic zipping bag. Pour juice over apples; toss well and drain. Cover bowl or seal bag; refrigerate until serving time. Serve dip with apple wedges. Makes about 16 servings.

Start a kitchen journal to note favorite recipes, family preferences, even special guests and celebrations. It'll make planning meals and parties much easier and is sure to become a cherished keepsake.

Kitchen Measurements

Equivalents

One gallon equals:
4 quarts • 8 pints • 16 cups • 128 fluid ounces

One quart equals:
2 pints • 4 cups • 32 fluid ounces

One pint equals:
2 cups • 16 fluid ounces

One cup equals:
8 fluid ounces • 16 tablespoons

1/2 cup equals:
8 tablespoons • 4 fluid ounces

1/4 cup equals:
4 tablespoons • 2 fluid ounces

1/8 cup equals:
2 tablespoons • 1 fluid ounce

One tablespoon equals:
3 teaspoons • 1/2 fluid ounce

Kitchen Substitutions

Ingredient	Quantity	Substitution
Baking powder	1 t.	1/3 t. baking soda + 2/3 t. cream of tartar
Baking soda	1 t.	2 t. baking powder, omit the salt in the recipe
Broth	1 c.	1 c. boiling water + 1 bouillon cube
Brown sugar	1 c.	1 c. sugar + 2 T. molasses
Butter	1 c.	1 c. margarine or 7/8 c. oil
Buttermilk	1 c.	1 T. white vinegar or lemon juice + enough milk to make 1 c., let stand 5 minutes
Baking chocolate, semi-sweet	1 oz.	3 T. baking cocoa + 3 T. sugar + 1 T. butter
Baking chocolate, unsweetened	1 oz.	3 T. baking cocoa + 1 T. butter
Cornstarch	1 T.	2 T. all-purpose flour
Egg	1 medium	1/4 c. egg substitute
Garlic	1 clove	1 t. minced garlic, or 1/8 t. garlic powder
Half-and-half	1 c.	3/4 c. milk + 1/3 c. melted butter
Herbs, fresh, chopped	1 T.	1 t. dried herbs
Lemon juice	1 T.	1-1/2 t. vinegar
Milk	1 c.	1/2 c. evaporated milk + 1/2 c. water
Onion, chopped	1 medium	2 T. dried, chopped onion or 1-1/2 t. onion powder
Sour cream	1 c.	1 c. plain yogurt or 1 c. cottage cheese, blended smooth
Sugar, granulated	1 c.	1-3/4 c. powdered sugar or 1 c. brown sugar, packed
Soy sauce	1 T.	1 T. Worcestershire sauce + 1 t. water
Tomato sauce	1 c.	3/4 c. tomato paste + 1/4 c. water
Vinegar	1 T.	2 T. lemon juice
Worcestershire sauce	1 T.	1 T. steak sauce
Yogurt	1 c.	1 c. cottage cheese + 1 t. lemon juice, blended smooth

INDEX

* Recipes with Variations

INDEX

★ Recipes with Variations

INDEX

* Recipes with Variations

Find Gooseberry Patch
wherever you are!

www.gooseberrypatch.com

Call us toll-free at 1·800·854·6673

ready in a jiffy · homemade in a hurry

Mom, when do we eat?

dinner's ready!

oh-so-easy eats · just a bite, please

U.S. to Metric Recipe Equivalents

Volume Measurements

1/4 teaspoon	1 mL
1/2 teaspoon	2 mL
1 teaspoon	5 mL
1 tablespoon = 3 teaspoons	15 mL
2 tablespoons = 1 fluid ounce	30 mL
1/4 cup	60 mL
1/3 cup	75 mL
1/2 cup = 4 fluid ounces	125 mL
1 cup = 8 fluid ounces	250 mL
2 cups = 1 pint =16 fluid ounces	500 mL
4 cups = 1 quart	1 L

Weights

1 ounce	30 g
4 ounces	120 g
8 ounces	225 g
16 ounces = 1 pound	450 g

Oven Temperatures

300° F	150° C
325° F	160° C
350° F	180° C
375° F	190° C
400° F	200° C
450° F	230° C

Baking Pan Sizes

Square		Loaf	
8x8x2 inches	2 L = 20x20x5 cm	9x5x3 inches	2 L = 23x13x7 cm
9x9x2 inches	2.5 L = 23x23x5 cm	Round	
Rectangular		8x1-1/2 inches	1.2 L = 20x4 cm
13x9x2 inches	3.5 L = 33x23x5 cm	9x1-1/2 inches	1.5 L = 23x4 cm